Ian Heaps on Fishing

Ian Heaps on Fishing

IAN HEAPS & COLIN MITCHELL

BUCHAN & ENRIGHT, PUBLISHERS
LONDON

First published in 1982 by
Buchan & Enright, Publishers, Limited
21 Oakley Street, London SW3 5NT

Copyright © Ian Heaps and Colin Mitchell 1982

All rights reserved. No part of this publication
may be reproduced, stored in a retrieval system,
or transmitted, in any form or by any means,
electronic, mechanical, photocopying, recording, or
otherwise, without the prior permission in writing
of the publishers.

ISBN 0 907675 02 6

Filmset by Inforum Ltd., Portsmouth
Printed in Great Britain by
Richard Clay (The Chaucer Press) Ltd,
Bungay, Suffolk

CONTENTS

	Introduction	ix
1	How I started	1
2	The people who influenced me	8
3	World Champion at the first attempt	12
4	My worst ever match	19
5	My best birthday present – the B & H title	23
6	The Southern Pole Championship	29
7	The best catch in the world	34
8	My favourite river	39
9	Learning from others	47
10	The England manager	51
11	Sponsored matches	55
12	Swimfeeder	61
13	How to use groundbait	65
14	Pole fishing	71
15	Popular floats	80
16	Sliding floats	86
17	Canals: the neglected fisheries	92
18	How to be a star	97
19	Preparing for matches	103
20	Life at the top	107

ILLUSTRATIONS

In matches everything is welcome*	3
Ian in 1969*	6
Kevin Ashurst at Coombe Abbey Lake	9
Ian nets a bream in the 1975 World Championships in Poland*	14
Ivan Marks has almost 100 lb of roach in his net†	16
The England team before the 1978 World Championships*	19
A bream taken by Ian during a practice session on the Erne†	25
Ian with part of his World record match catch†	26
Mark Downes with a 100 lb plus catch†	27
Dick Carr	30
Ken Collings	32
Ian in action on the River Blackwater in Ireland†	36
Ian with Private John Aitken*	38
Ian carefully unhooks a roach*	40
Ian wins his section on the Trent with this net of fish*	41
Ian fishing overdepth on the Trent*	45
Ian attracts a crowd wherever he fishes nowadays*	49
Stan Smith before the 1976 World Championships in Bulgaria*	52
The 1976 England team in Bulgaria*	53
Steve Gardener nets a bream	56
Ian puts another chub safely into the net*	57
Benny Ashurst, one of England's greatest anglers (*Dave Houghton*)	59
Ian holding several 'cannonballs' of feed . . .*	66
. . . and using them to bait his swim*	67
Ian watches as his 1977 World catch is weighed*	69
Ian in action with a carbon pole on the River Bann†	78
Various different kinds of floats*	82–83
Ian's float box*	89
Maggot ace Dave Thomas*	99
John Dean*	101
Ian's tackle box	105
Ian demonstrating how to fish with an improvised rod*	109

* Photos by Rodney Coldron
† Photos by courtesy of the Northern Ireland Tourist Board

INTRODUCTION

There are, in my opinion, three different types of angler. They range from those who are naturally brilliant, those who learn with practice and hard work, and the angler who enjoys himself every time he ventures out – although he will never become a very skillful angler.

I have been lucky enough to fish with many of the country's big-name anglers. And, thanks to the likes of Ivan Marks, Kevin Ashurst, Billy Makin, Dave Thomas, Ray Mumford and countless others, I have learnt a great deal about our sport.

When I was asked to help Ian put this book together I regarded him as one of our country's best. He had to be when you remember that he was only the third angler from this country to win the World Championship, after Billy Lane and Robin Harris. What I didn't realise was just how good Ian is.

He is one of those naturally brilliant anglers who possess what many refer to as 'fish sense'. Ian can tell when to change his methods to suit the fishing, but he can do it without having to really think about it. After a few trips out with him anyone would be a better angler. He makes everything look so simple that you wonder why he hasn't won everything in sight. That, of course, is due to the high standard of competition around and the unfairness of match fishing when you need to rely on a good draw.

One trip I made with Ian was to an England practice session on the River Blackwater in Northern Ireland. Ian decided to drop into a spot above a road bridge with Birmingham's Mark Downes above him, his big pal Kevin Ashurst just below him and Southerner Dickie Carr last man down. Ian tackled up a long pole with a heavy float and a lot of lead down the line, and handed it to me while he got the rest of his tackle together. Immediately, I hit into a good roach and then quickly followed with another. I admit that it was a good swim, but the fact that he had tackled it right from the off was enough to convince me of the great skill he has. For the record, both Mark and Kevin on either side of us, who to be fair didn't have such good spots, had to change methods before they really got stuck into the fish.

The following day, the day of the international, it would have been very easy for Ian and the rest of his colleagues to go on what they had learnt in practice and try to fish with long poles. They didn't. Instead, it was heavy wagglers and big sliders from the off – and England went on to win the match. Ian, fishing with one of his favourite sliders, won his section easily, and his weight was big enough to win the sections on either side of him. The look on his face throughout the match was enough to say everything – he knew he was going to score maximum points!

One of Ian's favourite haunts is the River Ribble and it was here that I met up with him one day to get more information for his story. Obviously, there was no way we were going to miss out on the chance of some fishing, so Ian dropped into a spot he liked the look of – even though he had never tried it before – and he put me in a noted spot.

It goes without saying that he was in to fish almost immediately, with chub and good dace on the caster. Having left me to fish with maggots, I was without a bite after a few hours' fishing and began to feel that Ian had pulled a fast one on me. But he insisted that I kept on flogging away at the spot. Eventually, fishing as he had told me, I hit into a small chub. Then the chub and dace kept coming until I ran out of bait. After borrowing more maggots from Ian I continued to catch until we couldn't see our floats any more.

I had tackled that swim exactly how Ian had told me. If I had been left to myself I would have tackled it differently – and although I am convinced I would have caught, I don't think I would have had the fish coming as readily.

Finally, I would like to point out that in compiling this book Ian has tried to include not only details of his great achievements, but also given some guidelines on how you can improve your fishing. There are plenty of books which tell you how to tackle up and tie your hooks. Very few books can help you catch fish when you are on the river bank. The best way to improve is to practise. As Ian says: 'The more you know the more you catch.'

COLIN MITCHELL

1
How I started

From the day I was born I think I must have been destined to be an angler. Both my father and grandfather were more than useful at the sport, and it was my Dad who started me off.

I was just five years old when he used to take me on my first trips to the Peak Forest Canal which was a short distance from our home in Stockport. At first he used to sit me on his basket and let me strike when he got a bite. I remember that we used to catch mostly roach with a few skimmer bream on bread using a rod and line.

It was those days on the canal that I reckon eventually helped me when I travelled further afield. We used to have to fish about three-quarters of the way over and I had to learn the tricks of concentrated feed.

Already at this stage my Dad was a household name amongst anglers. People just didn't travel to matches then like they do now and he established himself by winning club matches and big Opens in the area. Among his best wins was the 1,000 peg County Palatine Open which earned him £80, a lot of money in those days. The following year he came second in the same match and he added a number of 800 peg and 1,000 peg victories to his haul, many on the River Weaver, which was then one of the best venues in the country.

Dad was a member of the Romiley Anglers club and because of this I became the club's first junior member, being allowed to join I believe because of the high esteem in which he was held. The club had coach outings every Sunday to places like the Trent, Severn and Welland and, when I was 14, it was on one of these trips that I got my first match win.

It came in a match between Romiley and Beeston on the River

Soar at Kegworth. As we got off the coach Dad pointed out three or four anglers in the Beeston team who were 'Nationals'. That is they fished the All-England event which meant that they had to be pretty good. Altgether there were 120 people taking part. There was a sweep on the two Romiley coaches and an overall pool on the match. Dad had to finance my pools then so he didn't put me in the overall one, just the coaches. After the weigh-in I learned I had won with 8–14–0. Dad got a lot of stick on the coach, because he was second with 5 lb and collected the overall pool that I hadn't been put into.

I kept on going on these club outings and eventually I got so much to grips with them that I was never out of the first three. It was then that Dad said I should go on the Open circuit. One of the reasons was, I think, that club attendances were dropping because of the same people scoring regularly and he had to do something about it as he was chairman.

This took me travelling a lot more and I won my first Open match at the first attempt on the Newark Dyke at a place called the Malt Kilns, a very popular spot in those days. Double drawing was still allowed then and some of the top anglers were able to get where they wanted by buying more pegs until they hit on the right one.

On the way to the match one of the cars broke down and made us late, but it didn't really matter as I could only afford the one draw. Having drawn I started off to the downstream end and noticed all of the top lads in the best area. I had never fished the Dyke before, so as I made my way to my peg I kept a close eye on what everyone else was tackling up with. The 12 people above me were all ready and had put on big floats set at about 10 feet of depth.

I thought this would be the method, so I put on a big stick float which had a cane base and a balsa top and took seven No. 4 shot. The match had been under way for about five minutes before I was ready to cast in, and I could see fish coming in from the off. Everyone was fishing the middle and catching roach about 3–6 oz. Afterwards, I remember reading in the paper about the match and they said I had won by 'judicious feeding'. What I did was to drop the feed shorter and shorter until in the last two hours I was catching under my rod top. Despite coming that close in I stuck to the same float and the last fish I had was about 13 oz. I

HOW I STARTED

finished with 13–15–12, half pound ahead of the great Benny Ashurst – and I was still only 18.

It was about this time that I joined Abbey Hey and teamed up with Tony Bielderman, Tony Knight and Ian Allcock. Just like me with Romiley, they were enjoying success within their club,

It's only a tiny bleak, but in matches everything is welcome

IAN HEAPS ON FISHING

but Abbey Hey were a bit more forward looking and used to have some of their coach trips to Open matches. The four of us became known as the Abbey Hey quartet. We used to travel all over the place. Tony Knight had an old VW and how we all used to get into that with our gear I will never know. It takes me all of my time to get my own tackle into a car now. It just goes to show how much simpler the tackle was then.

Our first main venue was the River Trent and the famous Saturday sweepstakes at Burton Joyce which are still being run today, though in those days it was Terry Dorman and Gerry Woodcock who organised the matches. I had five wins there and eventually Tony Bielderman, who was responsible for booking tickets for matches for us, decided that we should now travel further afield.

We had fished the Severn but never really made an impact, so it was decided that we should fish there, the Witham, Welland and the Fenland system. At one Severn match, on the Quarry and County ground stretch, the four of us did exceptionally well in a 150 peg Open with three 50 peg sections.

Tony Bielderman was first in his section and won the match. I won the middle section and was second in the match whilst Ian was second in my section and third overall and Tony Knight won his section finishing fifth in the event. We won a few more on the Severn, and in one team match at Bewdley we took first and second placings using the wasp grub.

Due to our, and others', success the grub was banned from many of the matches on the river two years later. We didn't agree with this; after all, the motive is to catch as many fish as possible and the bait is there and available for anyone who is willing to collect it. Anyway we decided it was time to move on again and it was now the Relief Channel for us.

This was a big float water which meant yet another change. We had started on quills on the canals, and moved through the stick float, medium balsas, heavy balsas and now onto wagglers and heavy sliders for distance fishing. Rudyard Lake – a local water to me – had produced a lot on the slider, and experience there helped me on the Relief Channel. In fact, it was here that I took my best ever match haul of roach in this country. I had 47 lb, including three fish for 2 lb, all on casters and a sliding float. There was just one hybrid in that haul.

HOW I STARTED

By this time I was 20 and had been practising for slider fishing for about 12 months when the big CIU National was due to be fished on the Relief Channel. I started to catch skimmers between 8 oz and 1¼ lb from the off in around 14 feet of water. I was casting out with about 8 feet of depth and counting to six as the bait dropped the rest of the way. The float would then slide straight away or lift.

Fish were coming steadily and I had a young lad sitting behind me to whom I was explaining the slider. I had just run out of my second bowl of groundbait and as I mixed the third I told this youngster to keep an eye on my float. I knew he had been very attentive so when he said I had a bite I just put the bowl down and without even looking struck into a fish. With one turn of the reel handle I was in contact with another bream – but I lost it as the line had been wrapped around the bale arm.

Everything went, my hook, shot, float . . . and the bream shoal. I tackled up again but just couldn't catch as the fish had moved and anglers about six pegs away were catching. Forty-five minutes later I got my first bite and with one and a half hours left the fish had returned, only now they were there in twice the numbers and that count of six as my float settled was very important. The fish were now taking more readily about three or four feet off the bottom, and if I left the tackle in longer than that count of six the fish were able to mouth the bait and then drop it without my knowing. Now, I realise that all I needed to do was to shallow off at about three feet and I could have spotted the bites easily. Anyway I ended up with 28 lb and finished third in the match.

Two months after that CIU match I was fishing a match on the tidal River Trent at Dunham Bridge when a Sheffield angler came up behind me and asked if I had lost a float during the CIU. He then held up that sliding float which had worked so well for me and I reached out to take it thinking he had brought it back. But to my surprise he snatched it back and said he wasn't going to give it up as it had won him two matches and helped him to second position twice over those two months during matches on the River Nene.

When I was just sixteen our family made a decision which put me into angling's record books – but could have also cost me the World Championship win. My father had just been made redundant from his job in the hat making business and we had decided to emigrate to Canada to join my mother's two sisters out there. Luckily, though, we only went for a two–year trial period and because we couldn't settle we returned to Stockport the day that time period was up.

But during our stay in Canada I landed the fish of a lifetime, a 50 lb carp. At the time, that was a record over there and it still beats our own British record by 6 lb. Fishing in De La Salle park in Hamilton, Ontario, I hooked the fish on worm and soon there was a crowd a few hundred strong watching the lengthy fight. I was fishing from a pier, so when the fish was eventually beaten I had to leave it to a policeman in a launch, who had also come to watch, to net the monster for me. What a contrast for me when I returned home to join those Abbey Hey lads. The Weaver, one of our favourite venues and a place stuffed with fish, had been ravaged by pollution. It was very sad and led to me starting that trek to the Trent, a water where casters could produce about 8 lb of fish for me on nearly every peg.

Even in 1969 Ian caught his fair share of fish

HOW I STARTED

It was shortly after my return home and teaming up with the Abbey Hey lads that we were all called up by Benny Ashurst for the Stoke City National team. The match that year was on the Trent and we started it as red-hot favourites. Well, we didn't let anyone down as we won; I remember coming well up in my section, although the match was then decided on weight and not points as now.

I had already fished Nationals for Chesire and County Palatine and only stayed with Stoke for two seasons. My second season saw me win my section for them on the Bristol Avon with 14 lb. Then, Stockport, my home town team, joined the National Federation of Anglers and joined the Second Division. Dad persuaded me to join the team and I fished their first match on the Relief Channel. It was a terrible match as I was drawn near Downham, but I managed just two eels and a perch to finish well up my section.

Still in the second division, Stockport travelled the following season to the Warwickshire Avon and made no mistake in getting promotion. There were a record number of teams fishing the match and the points total we set can never be broken unless there is ever another National with so many taking part – and that is now unlikely with the number of divisions now run by the NFA.

That match also saw me in action with the slider, taking 13 lb of quality roach from about 17 feet of water to win my section.

2
The people who influenced me

Obviously, there are a great number of people who have influenced me during my fishing career, but the one person whom I must credit with most of my success is my father, Jim.

I remember when I was just a very young lad, that the River Mersey ran about half a mile away from the back of our house and, just as it is now, it was a polluted, filthy river devoid of any life – never mind fish. Dad used to show me what would be a chub swim and why, where the barbel and bream would be, where the bends and deeps were, and where the roach would lie.

So, even though that river was so dirty that it was no use to anyone, I knew exactly where each species could be found if they had been there. Without doubt, that sort of education from my father, who was a naturalist, helped me to lay the foundations on which to build my own knowledge as I grew older, and gave me the basis of becoming a good angler.

I am one of the lucky people who has an inborn talent for looking at a river and weighing up form – I suppose it comes from those early days of learning everything about a waterway. As I became older and able to weigh things up for myself it was great to have talks with my father who would probably see things in a slightly different light. It really is like watching two people fishing totally differently and then coming out with another formula for fishing their swims, but one which is totally right.

I think it is of the utmost importance that someone should have a person around with whom they can exchange information. If you go to an Open match you will always notice that the anglers who never get on are the ones who are rapidly on their way home. The ones who get on – whether they have won a prize that day or not – are the ones who stay behind at the headquarters listening to

Kevin Ashurst swings in a small perch at Coombe Abbey Lake near Coventry

the successful anglers telling how they scored.

Those anglers are full of themselves. It doesn't matter whether they were first, second or third; ask them how they caught their fish and they will tell you in every detail. There is a lot of valuable information swapped whilst waiting for the prize distribution. Anyone who wants to get on in match fishing should spare that short time to hang on and learn how those fish have been caught.

As long as my father is alive we will still talk about fishing. It is surprising that when I think he hasn't got a lot more to offer me, he will come up with an idea right out of the blue. When there is something I have not been able to get to the bottom of, he has come up with an idea and made it all so clear. I'm blessed with a father who has got this gift and the only person I know in a similar situation is my pal Kevin Ashurst and his father Benny.

It's amazing that the old hands like Benny and my father have still got this intuition which can be called on when it is needed. I would like to think that over the years Kevin and I have also helped each other with a few ideas, and I am always willing to swap information with him. I enjoy travelling to competitions with him and our ideas are usually similar. For instance, at the moment we are both into the bloodworm fishing scene.

One of the things about bloodworm fishing is having the bait just half an inch off the bottom. I visited a local water recently to find out how much feed I could put in, as it varies from day to day. It is only now that I am starting to sense when to put a lot of feed in and when not to. Kevin is in exactly the same race at the moment. This day I caught fish the normal way, but found I could also catch by putting the bait three inches off the bottom, which was a new way as far as I was concerned.

I found that I caught fish like this – it was in the winter – when I just couldn't get fish half an inch off bottom. Talking to Kevin on the way to a match I found that he had discovered exactly the same thing at his own local reservoir. It's funny how you can find something out yourself and then, by talking to someone who is as equally involved as you, find they have found the same thing. This gives the pair of you added confidence in the method you have found.

It's very difficult to say who has influenced me as I respect all good anglers. I could even go as far to say I respect all anglers because you can learn something from nearly everybody. One of the secrets of the game is to always have your ears pinned back and listen to conversations about angling as there is always something that comes out of them that might clear up one of your own problems or help out where you have been derailed.

If I had to name the anglers who have influenced me then I would fill a book with names alone. I'm prepared to listen to anyone and fishing is a game where you are forever learning. If you cease to learn you will have to take a seat in the background.

A lot of people believe that many of the top anglers reach their prime when they are in their thirties. Well, I was around that age when I won the World Championship but, to be fair, that was the first time I had been picked and I think that I reached my prime in the middle twenties. I think one of the important things in being a successful match angler is to have an active mind and to be ready to think one step ahead all the time.

Once your mind becomes less active then your methods are less numerous. Generally speaking, I think that an angler should have enough information, and be mature enough, to be at the top when he is about 30. If he is physically and mentally fit there is no reason why he should not stay at the very top until he is about 40. Something which is never talked about in angling is keeping fit, but I think that if someone looked after themselves their angling would benefit.

3

World Champion at the first attempt

Imagine being called on by your country for the first time to fish in the World Championship and then winning the title with a new record weight. Well, that's just what happened to me and you can understand why my Dad wouldn't believe it when he was first told!

It all began whilst I was fishing a match on the River Welland. I was catching roach steadily when I heard a car door slam behind me. When I looked around the England manager, Stan Smith, was climbing through the fence and the next thing I knew he had introduced himself and offered me a place in his team.

When he asked how I felt about representing England in Poland I nearly fell off my basket and, in fact, I never caught another fish in that match. I wasn't really suprised by the call, just the timing of it; I had been fishing really well four years previously and could have perhaps expected it then. Not wanting to cause a fuss I had just plodded on and I believed that when I got my call it could quite easily have been my colleague Tony Knight who would have got a place as his form was the best in the North West.

Stan had approached me a couple of months before the match and at that stage I was just one of the six man squad; I could still be the unlucky angler left on the sidelines. I went out on half a dozen practice sessions and spent a lot of time practising methods on local waters which I believed were similar to the Bydgoszcz Canal where we would be fishing.

I spent hours on Compstall Reservoir just working at fishing different depths. Dozens of weighted sliders and other floats occupied a lot of my time at home as I put the finishing touches to them for the match, and I spent hours just throwing balls of

WORLD CHAMPION AT THE FIRST ATTEMPT

groundbait until I could put them all onto one spot.

We had two practice sessions on the water before the Championship which had proved invaluable. On the first we caught very little, but on the second we found the fish at the bottom on the two shelves on either side of the canal. This meant the far shelf was out of reach of the pole angler as was the middle where there appeared to be no fish. However, it wasn't until the night before the event that I knew I was in the team.

Now I am not a nervous person, but that match was a nailbiter for me. On my third cast in I got my first bite and missed it! Immediately I re-cast and hooked the first fish of the event, a roach about $2\frac{1}{2}$ oz which brought a big shout from the spectators who were lining the far bank. I wound that roach straight in and swung it to my chest. Looking back I suppose I should have netted it as I just didn't know then how the match was going to go.

The next cast brought another roach from the far shelf, then the lock gates which controlled the venue were opened and it was just too fast to fish the far line. I had to come in to the near shelf. I was using the same tackle as I had over the far side, a big waggler with plenty of lead down the line. I used 2 lb hook length with a 3 lb reel line and a forged No. 18 hook baited with maggots even though we fed casters.

After about ten minutes the flow started to ease off again and I had my first fish close in, a bream around 12 oz. I kept fishing the near line for another ten minutes whilst putting bait into that far swim. I went back over and took a roach straight away. The following cast produced a lovely sail-away bite which I thought was the bottom until it started to move.

It was then I realised I had hooked one of the carp that were in the canal. My heart beat faster and faster because I knew I had to keep within the markers which separated my peg from the adjoining ones. If the fish went over those imaginary marks on the water and was spotted by a steward I might as well snap it off for it would not count. Immediately I stuck my rod under the water so that it couldn't be spotted.

Now the only problem with that was that I didn't know where the fish was either! Then I realised that I had to land the carp to ensure a good section placing for the team. I remembered reading in the angling papers how, the year before, three or four of the England team had lost carp during that match and I thought to myself that this particular year it would not read that Ian Heaps had lost one. From then on I played that fish as if my life depended on it.

Even when I had the fish in my landing net my worries were not over. During the match we were not allowed to use keepnets, and I had to transfer the fish from the landing net into the plastic receptacle that was my holding bag. Now this sounds easy enough – except when I tell you that these plastic bags were on metal frames and I had snapped my frame at the start when I tried to position it. This meant the wire loop holding the bag was just shoved into the wicker of my basket. Finally though, that 3 lb fish was in the bag and I had re-baited and cast back in.

It was then that my left hand started trembling and it took me three attempts to put the double gozzer maggot on to the hook. On the first two attempts I burst both maggots. By this time there were thousands of people on the opposite bank and everyone of

Ian nets a bream in the 1975 World Championships in Poland. A vast crowd gathered on the other side of the Bydgoszcz Canal

them must have applauded as I landed the carp – the noise was tremendous.

Back into the water went that float and it lifted half an inch immediately. It must be on the shelf, I thought to myself. I struck for safety and was into a bream around 3 lb and that was the end of the nerves as that fish slid smoothly into the waiting landing net. I was on my way and that crowd was now behind me and willing me on. Every fish was greeted by a round of applause and cheers and I returned the compliment by acknowledging them by raising my arm.

Several times I had false bites as I inadvertantly pulled the bottom end only float under myself. Every one of that crowd wanted me to strike, so I had to make a big show of proving to them that it was my fault and not another fish. Eventually, the whistle went for the end and I shall never forget the shouting and clapping that followed and the cries of 'Bravo' from the crowd that not only lined the opposite bank but were even up the trees trying to get a better vantage view.

I felt about nine feet tall because I had every confidence that I had won my section and not let the team down. Little did I know then that I had won the match. If it had been a match at home I would have thought I had won, but I never believed I had won the World match at the first attempt. There was bound to have been someone else catching like me.

Now all the fish have to be counted and weighed at the end and the first person behind me was manager Stan Smith who knew I was in with a chance of the individual crown. This was when problem number one came. All the fish were tipped out of the bag but the rules say if any are covered in dirt they will not count. Luckily Stan managed to throw a piece of canvas over the cinder track just as the fish were being tipped out. Thirty minutes after that I knew I had won. Everyone was shaking my hand and Ivan Marks, who had been in the next section to me for England, was the first of my team-mates that I saw.

I just couldn't believe it when they said I was the champion. I fell to my knees and my first thoughts were what my Dad would be thinking back home if he knew. Later, at the presentation, it was just all too much to imagine. It was like a dream. There was a massive hall full of stone statues, big pillars and polished floors – just the type of place to crown a World Champion. All the

The weigh-in after an International and Ivan Marks has almost 100 lb of roach in his net

WORLD CHAMPION AT THE FIRST ATTEMPT

announcements were made in several languages, except English, so I only knew they wanted me when a girl came to escort me to the rostrum and they played the National Anthem.

It was the proudest moment of my life to stand up there for two minutes whilst the rest of the teams listened in silence to 'God Save The Queen', but the only sad part was that I wasn't able to telephone home. My Dad had fished the River Trent that day and evidently as soon as he got home the phone never stopped ringing as friends tried to find out how I had got on.

It was beyond my Dad's wildest dreams that I should win, so when Manchester journalist Don Bridgewood, an old friend, rang him and congratulated him on being the father of the World Champion he thought it was just a big joke. But as Don went into detail about how I had set a new event weight record and how the team had finished second overall he started to believe it.

The news spread like wildfire and for three weeks our telephone was red-hot with good wishes and congratulatory calls. The first time I was able to ring home was when I touched down at Heathrow with the rest of the team, but when I arrived home it was champagne all round with friends and neighbours sharing the glory.

Even the customs men at the airport helped in the celebrations. After leaving my special safe seat on the plane I was given VIP treatment and allowed to skip customs because I had a giant pot vase which became mine with the title.

For the record, I finished that World event with eight bream, two carp and four roach for 10,220 grammes, about 22 lb 8½ oz, to beat the old record set in 1972 by a Dutchman. He had taken 20 lb 5½ oz in the match in Czechoslovakia. The rest of the team that day was Kevin Ashurst, Ivan Marks, Tony Scott and Terry Payne.

Now a lot of people ask me if England are capable of winning the World Championship – second in the team event was the closest we had been up to that date, and we were just pipped by a Frenchman who had a late rally with the fish. Well, my answer to these people is that given the right venue we can easily take this title.

Just look at the class of angler we have in this country besides those I have already mentioned. Forgetting the great old timers like Benny Ashurst and one of our other World Champions, Billy Lane, we still have greats like Robin Harris, who is England's only other World master, John Illingworth, Clive Smith, Ken Giles, Tom Pickering, Denis White and countless others who I hope will forgive me for not being able to get all of their names in.

The only thing that spoils our chances are the rules which favour the Continental styles, the restricted line, no legering and the advantage small fish have over the bigger ones because of the points system. One of the things I would like to see introduced is the allowing of practice sessions on the match stretch, for in too many of these events we have found a great difference between it and the practice stretch.

4
My worst ever match

Besides my World title victory there are two other matches which I am never ever going to forget. One was on the Great Ouse near Cambridge and the other is the World match in Austria where England finished last. However, that match in Austria will not go down as one of my worst; I reckon it is one of the best I have ever fished, even though I only ended up with just one bite for my troubles.

I am still convinced that had the conditions not changed dras-

The England team in Vienna before the 1978 World Championships on the Danube

tically, practically overnight, England would have notched up their first ever win on that fateful day. The water suited us down to the ground. A practice session earlier in the week had also given us the confidence we needed. Young Mark Downes from Birmingham landed a good carp and Tommy Pickering from Barnsley had a netful of decent fish. We knew the venue suited our running line tactics with waggler or sliding floats and we were eagerly awaiting the match.

But when the match day came the water had stopped flowing and there was no wind. The big fish would not feed in those conditions and, as usual, the tiddler snatchers from the Continent had a field day. I am still convinced that our gamble was right. Using our own tactics we had the chance of a soar-away victory, but we would have had little chance of beating those foreigners at their own game.

Now, as for that other match, I just wish that I could eliminate it from my brain completely. Looking back on my lengthy match fishing career, I just cannot remember any match which led to so many nightmares for me. I can safely say, in fact, that it was my worst ever match.

This was an invitation match on the Ouse between top anglers, television stars and personalities. Bill Maynard, television's Selwyn Froggett, Dick Ward and my other Stockport team colleague Alan Mayer, were three of those involved.

There was also a French team. It was the first time I had seen a French team in action with their heavy bombardment of groundbait at the start of a match and I was about 20 years old at the time. I had been to the river for a practice before the event so when the day came and I drew right in the same area I was pretty happy. During practice I had taken some quality fish, including bream and chub, fishing right against the weeds which were sticking up out of the water on the far bank.

My peg had the weeds on the far bank but between me and the Frenchman – who was drawn next to me – there was a bed of cane-type weeds which were about six to eight feet deep. Then there was a nice clean sandy bed forming a bay and this is where I stood, in the water. On the far bank the reeds also formed a series of bays. It looked really 'chubby' and I had a big bet with the bookie because I had pleasure-fished the same area and I was full of confidence.

MY WORST EVER MATCH

Well, the match started and, for the first time in my life, I saw the Frenchman heave in 30 or 40 balls of groundbait, about a third of the way out. I just couldn't believe what I was seeing – especially when he caught a small roach on his first cast! As it happens, he didn't catch a lot more during the match. Meanwhile, I put one small ball of groundbait, laced with casters, to the far bank.

I was floatfishing the peg, and my first fish was a skimmer bream which was followed by a little chub and then a roach. I was expecting a perch, bleak and then a gudgeon as my next fish, because I seemed to be catching one of every species. Suddenly though, I hit a chub of about 1½ lb. It came in nice and safe and I netted it.

Then the problems started. I had my basket in front of me as a table top and the keepnet in front of that. On my left was a bait holder on a bank stick, on my right was the bed of weeds between me and the Frenchman. It was then that I hooked a chub of about 4 lb. Well, it swam straight at me and *wham*, it was in those weeds. I could see the fish and was trying to shovel it out with the landing net. The weed was laying across it, but I could still see its huge silver side and I just couldn't get it out. The hook eventually came back with the shank bent at right angles. That was catastrophe number one.

I cast across again, and within four throws over I latched onto another chub, this time around the 2 lb mark. That again came right in front of me but this time, just as I was going to net it, it shot forwards, hit my wellington, swam around the bank stick holding the bait tray and off it went. Goodbye to fish number two.

I'm not kidding you, I just couldn't believe it. Out I went again and caught another about 1 lb plus a smaller one. Then I hooked one about 3 lb and brought it in, carefully guiding it slowly past all of these rushes and other objects. In front of me was that lovely sandy bank with a clean bottom as far as I could see. The chub was now well clear of those weeds so I was just letting it swim over the sand until it was tired enough to bring to the top.

All of a sudden the line just went as fast as it could be. It had snagged up on the bank where I thought there wasn't anything to trouble me. Impossible, I thought. Later on, though, I saw what the problem was. The river was controlled by lock-gates and the level was altering a foot or so as these were opened and closed.

IAN HEAPS ON FISHING

When the river dropped to its lowest there, on that sandy bank, was one single plant, one of those which looks like a cabbage.

I caught a few more fish, then I lost one about $1\frac{1}{2}$ lb which flipped out of my hands as I was putting it into the keepnet. The last one I lost was in the dying minutes of the match, and to make things worse it happened just as a crowd had gathered behind me.

Despite all of the other problems of the day I hadn't been caught up on the bottom as I trotted through and all the bites had come from one particular spot. As my float went past it this time it slipped away, I struck and I was fast on the bottom – or so I thought.

I said to the crowd: 'Would you believe it, I haven't been caught up there all day.' I was just pulling for the break when it started to move. It went down the river at walking pace and I started wondering what I had hooked as I had the job of bringing it all that way upstream, knowing that there was the big bed of rushes between it and me.

Wading out as far as I could I stuck my rod right out so that I had the leverage to pull the fish out of the obstruction. As I started to tow the fish gently upstream it came quietly until it was into the weeds. I waded out of the water, walked down the bank, and reeled in the line until I was level with the fish.

Now, I could see where the line was going into the water and spotted it wrapped around a big branch. I waded in up to my waist and freed it from the branch. Then there was this big splash just like a bomb had been dropped and the fish was off. My tackle was broken into pieces and I still don't know what I had hooked.

I finished with 7 lb 14 oz and the match was won with four chub for 13 lb. I ended up just out of the money and the team – on which we had also had a big bet – was second, just a few pounds behind the winners. I wasn't a very popular fellow. That has just got to be my worst match.

5
My best birthday present – the B & H Title

The present I got for my 34th birthday went down in the record books! It came in the form of a then new five-hour match world record of 166 lb 11½ oz taken in the 1977 Benson and Hedges Festival fished on the River Erne at Enniskillen in Northern Ireland.

That net full of roach, plus a few bream, took my total catch over the festival's three days to 318 lb 8½ oz and won the series for me. It was an incredible week's fishing, especially when you think that the monster catch came on the final day.

Yet after the first day's match when I only had 22 lb on my score card, things looked bad, especially when I heard that Billy Knott junior, that Cockney character now living in Cornwall, had taken 125 lb of roach. At first I just couldn't believe it. How could anyone catch that amount of roach in a match? I had to keep asking myself.

Ask me now and I will predict even bigger weights in matches over there than you will think possible. Up to 220 lb of roach and over 300 lb of bream are within reach if the right angler gets on the right peg and can pace himself and his feed properly over the five hours.

To understand why the catches on the Erne are so high you have to understand just how many fish there are. I am convinced that the shoals of bream are gigantic, and at the time of year they fish the Bensons (May) most of the roach in the Erne system are passing through the match length because of the spawning period. I think that in some pegs the roach are so thick on the ground that when they take a bait they don't register a good bite because they can't move very far.

Getting back to that world shattering Bensons, it was only on the second day, a practice session, that I realised what the secret was. There was a shelf close in on some pegs up to about six feet deep, and this was where the roach lived. Go over that ledge into the deeper water and the chances were that you were among the bream.

Now remember that this is a match and the best way to get a big weight fast is to go after the roach and the roach/bream hybrids. These fish weigh less than the big bream but they come much faster and can be handled that much easier. However, if you manage to get in a position where fishing is like this, do not forget those bream are there, they can come in handy if the roach decide they have had enough for a while.

Now came the day of the second match and, armed with what I thought was the right information, I set off for my peg on Irvine's Island near the centre of Enniskillen. I tackled up with a four metre pole and tied 4 lb line direct to the crook with no elastic shock absorber. On went a 2½ lb trace with a No. 14 semi-barbless hook for speed and better hooking of fish. The float had a bristle insert so that I could see bites easily and had a bulk shot of 3 AA to get the bait down to the fish with a tell tale between that and the hook.

I plumbed up the depth and discovered I had the five to six feet that I needed. Next lesson I learnt was about the feeding pattern. The more I threw in the faster the fish came, only the more I put in the more the big fish went to the bottom and I found that the smaller roach were intercepting my hookbait on its way down.

At the end of that day I had 130 lb compared to the 60 lb the peg had produced on the first session, and what pleased me more was that I had beaten an angler nearby who had been catching bream steadily. The reason was that my fish had come faster and I had been taking up to eight roach every minute. On that second day, though, Croydon angler John McCarthy had taken 140 lb of roach from Billy Knott's first day peg to put me into second spot. Overall, I was lying in sixth position and I was 50 lb adrift of the leaders.

The Friday was the last day of the festival and I knew there was a possibility that I could win when I pulled a peg in H section, once again in the town, out of the hat. I set up the same pole rig and a rod and line as soon as I got there. As soon as the whistle went in went the feed and I cast out with the rod. Immediately I

MY BEST BIRTHDAY PRESENT

had a fish and that rod was discarded for the pole.

From then on it was all hard work. In the first hour a spectator reckoned I had taken around 75 lb, but I wasn't so confident as I knew a lot of the fish were in the 2 oz bracket. At the end my hands were cut to pieces and covered in blood, the results of

A nice bream taken by Ian during a practice session on the Erne, in the centre of Enniskillen

where hooks had pulled into my skin as I ran my hand down the line and over the fish to unhook it. But when the fish went on the scales I had that 166 lb 11½ oz, enough to beat the old record set by Loughborough's Tom Bedder by 6 lb 11½ oz.

The amount of bait I used that last day can only be called phenomenal and I reckon it cost me almost £20. I emptied a baby's bath full of groundbait into that swim around three times and included in that feed was ten pints of hemps, a gallon of casters and 12 pints of maggots.

Now if, after reading that, you think fishing among this number of fish is as easy as it sounds, let me let you into a secret – it isn't. The following year's Benson and Hedges, won by my pal Kevin Ashurst of Leigh, produced more 100 lb plus weights, but you didn't need half as much feed in many of the pegs.

I believe this was due to there being less roach on the match length, and the same is true the year after Kevin's win when my

Ian with part of the catch from the River Erne that gave him the World record match catch

The River Bann is one of Ian's favourite venues. This 100 lb plus catch was taken by team-mate Mark Downes

other Stockport colleague, Bill Reade, won the event. To keep those fish coming it was necessary to scale down the feed. In fact we found that on some pegs it was best to cut out the groundbait altogether and just use loose feed casters. This way you could still take the big weights of roach even though the shoals were not as big as before. The reason behind this was that whereas before you could afford to put a lot of feed in because of the head of roach, now you had to introduce just enough so as not to overfeed the smaller number. Also, as I have mentioned before, it helps to keep the bigger fish coming.

Now, you might be thinking that all this sounds great – if you are fishing the Benson or another Irish river stuffed full of fish. But, believe me, the same principle applies to wherever you are fishing. You must feed according to how many fish there are and how they are feeding.

Most anglers have now heard of the River Bann at Portadown in Northern Ireland, which, for me, is one of the finest roach waters in Europe. At times when you are fishing there you would swear there are so many fish you could walk across the river on their backs. Knowing this you would expect to have to pile in the maggots and groundbait. On some occasions you would score, but not always.

Some of the locals can catch three-figure weights of roach on just two pints of maggots and the minimum amount of groundbait, and that isn't because there are so many fish you don't need to feed! The maggots are put straight to the bottom with a bait dropper to get the big fish interested. Then, they drop in small amounts of bread which brings up the small fish away from their feed. With a big bunch of shot just near their hook they can get straight through to the bigger specimens and knock their monster weights up in next to no time! It is a simple tactic – but then most of the answers to what appear complex fishing problems are usually easy.

6

The Southern Pole Championship

One of the most satisfying matches I can ever remember winning was the Southern Pole Championships on the River Lea at Broxbourne in Hertfordshire. It contained a very strong line up of many of the best pole anglers in the country and was organised by Gerry Casey, the promoter of the famous Southern Top Twenty.

I had only fished the river once before but I had done my homework and decided on the method. I rang up my England team colleague Dickie Carr before the match because I knew this was his local venue and he could tell me how it was fishing. Dick told me that the odd skimmer bream to around the 1 lb mark had been showing, and that made up my mind for me.

Knowing how much those skimmers like bloodworms I decided to heave plenty of bloodworm and joker feed into my peg from the off just like the continentals. I had drawn reasonably well, opposite the swimming baths on the well-known Conkers stretch, but heard that Dick and that other good Hertfordshire bleak angler Ade Scutt had drawn well just below the Crown bridge and were on bleak.

I had a very comfortable bank with weeds on the far bank and at my feet. I chose to fish about three parts of the way across where it was about seven feet deep – just a fraction deeper than anywhere else in the swim. It was at this point I decided to heave in 30 balls of feed, an unknown tactic on this venue.

I started fishing then and got bites immediately from bleak which had gone down onto my feed. I caught about a dozen bleak but wasn't happy about it because I knew I could have caught them faster off the top than from the bottom. Also, I was fishing with an olivette on my line with the idea of getting through those bleak to get at the better quality fish which were down below.

Dick Carr, whose information on the Lea helped Ian win the Southern Pole Championships

THE SOUTHERN POLE CHAMPIONSHIP

Those bigger fish moved in quickly though. Within about ten minutes I had a roach of about 8 oz and this was followed by a string of small roach between 3 and 4 oz and a few perch. Then, what I was really looking for came . . . a skimmer bream of about 10 oz. This was followed by another and another and another . . . plus the odd roach in between.

A few of these roach were 8–10 oz and were taken on three bloodworms on a No. 16 hook to 1.7 lb line. Now this in itself is a lesson to some people. They think that pole fishing is all small hooks and light lines, but it doesn't have to be. The tackle I used here was needed because I knew there were one or two good fish about, and I didn't want to lose any of them.

From then on I caught steadily, roach and skimmers plus a chub which I had to net. Then, about an hour from the end of the five-hour match bites started to trail off and I knew those fish had eaten everything I had put in at the start. I had made a mistake! Looking back at it now I know that I should have thrown 40 balls at them immediately.

I didn't want to put any more feed in at that stage because I had seen the effect this had in the past. Sometimes you can get away with it, but most of the time the fish just disappear as the food falls on their backs. At this stage though there was about 45 minutes left and I was either going to sit there and get another four fish or take a gamble and hope they came back.

I decided to put as much bloodworms and jokers as I could in ball of feed and make up three small balls. This way there would be the maximum amount of feed possible getting straight down to those fish. There was as much feed in those three small balls as the equivalent in five of the cannon ball size ones I had put in to start with.

These balls were absolutely solid and were packed heavily with soil so they would go straight down. I put them in one on top of the other and kept my fingers crossed that the gamble would pay off. Twenty minutes passed without a bite and I thought to myself: 'Ian, you've had it.'

But then the float dipped and I was into a skimmer again. This was followed quickly by another and they came steadily to the end of the match to give me a total of just over 8 lb and victory by just over 3 oz from the second placed angler.

Now all of those fish had come from a swim about 30 feet out

Ken Collings who regularly swaps information with Ian

THE SOUTHERN POLE CHAMPIONSHIP

from the bank, but I had been lucky it was only shallowish. This had enabled me to fish with just nine feet of line from the pole top and then unship a few sections of pole every time I caught a fish.

To give you some idea of the other conditions on the day I will tell you that it was very fine – and that brought out the crowds to watch how to tackle the Lea with a pole. But weather also brought out the boats, and it is no fun having to manoeuvre your float between the rowing boats as they go past.

One thing that this match should teach you though is how effective the continental system of heavy groundbaiting can be, especially with the bloodworm. And I am not talking about its use just on a canal or stillwater. Here I had put it to good effect on a river, and there is no reason why, given the right conditions, it should not work on other flowing waters.

Finally I would like to thank Ken Collings of Dorking for helping me – unknowingly – to win this match. It was Ken who first persuaded me to start travelling South to try out some of their interesting matches.

After the pole match I was really glad of his advice – but when you think about it how could I have refused it? After all, how do you ignore a man with such a fine record, which includes the River Trent match catch record in 1978?

7

The best catch in the world

One of my best ever catches on rod and reel came in just four hours of fabulous fishing in Sweden during an exploratory trip to that country.

It was a river called the Ronne at a place called Skaldervicken which produced sport that I shall never forget. It was a very scenic setting, just where the river entered the sea, but there was no tide. I went to the water with two Swedish journalists with the intention of finding the ide, a fish which looks very much like a chub but has a carp's mouth.

They can grow to six or seven pounds, although we didn't find them that big in our swims which were about four feet deep. We had them up to about $4\frac{1}{2}$ lb and I had 175 lb of them in four hours. Most of the fish in that catch were around $1\frac{1}{2}$ to 2 lb.

It was a very windy day and as the water was shallow I decided to ledger fish it with bread, but after an hour I hadn't had a fish whilst the Swede on the next peg, fishing with worm on the float, had taken four of these ide. I thought to myself that worm must be the answer, so I changed to that bait and still didn't get a fish. He was still catching a fish or two so I decided to have a go on my favourite waggler.

On the waggler I had a fish on the very first cast with a worm and realised that these fish were a foot off the bottom. So, I ended up fishing three feet deep, and although I caught on worm it became evident with every additional ball of cloud groundbait that the fish came thicker into the swim – and whilst I was catching a fish about every fourth run down I changed to bread and that was when the magic started.

I broke up three or four loaves of bread into the groundbait – even though on the lead I hadn't been able to catch on the bread, having been forewarned that this was the bait. Finally though, I was in the swing of things with the waggler fishing about five rod lengths out with size 10 and 12 hooks baited with a big chunk of flake and all of the shot – 3BB bulked near the hook with one and a half swan shot to weight the float.

It was the simplest type of fishing you could want and it was only the second time I had caught these ide. The previous occasion was just a short way up-river fishing with a big double rubber balsa float which also accounted for some roach and bream.

Now the more food I threw at these fish the faster they seemed to come, and they put up a great fight on a prototype carbon fibre road I was trying out. It had a very stiff action and really killed these fish and helped to quieten them quickly, a point which really pleased me.

In fact, I changed about half-way through to an ordinary glass rod and it took me twice as long to get the fish in.

Now when you consider that these fish have a similar fighting power to that of a chub or carp you can imagine how I felt after that hectic four-hour session. At that time it was my best catch on rod and line in that space of time, although I had taken bream catches over longer periods of time, of 160 lb and 180 lb on the float in consecutive weekends at Lochmaben in Dumfriesshire.

Now that was one of the best catches I have ever had, but since then I have become a regular visitor to Northern Ireland and I maintain that the quality of fishing over there cannot be beaten. Here, you can catch so many 150 lb plus catches in so many areas that it is just out of this world.

Let me tell you now how I first got involved with going to Northern Ireland. In fact, I can reveal that at first I was always wary of going. I went quite regularly to the South, to the Ballinasloe Festivals, had a great time there and got some good catches of bream and rudd, but unfortunately no roach and I really like to catch this species.

When I heard that the Benson and Hedges people were staging their first festival in Northern Ireland with big prize money, it wasn't only the prize money which looked lucrative. For I heard that the match was going to be on the River Erne, and although I had never been I knew of its record as a roach water and I fancied going.

IAN HEAPS ON FISHING

Now this was in 1976, the same year as I was the reigning World Champion, and while I had made arrangements to go on this trip, a very good friend of mine and a very well-known angler said to me: 'Ian, don't you think you are sticking your neck out a little bit going to Northern Ireland in your position.' I didn't really understand what he meant at first but then he emphasised that if there was going to be any trouble in the province then I could be at the centre of it as my name was in the limelight at the time.

Well, I shrugged all that off, then, a few weeks later, another friend came up to me and said the same thing. Then someone else said it, and another, and I started to think and decided that I shouldn't become involved. I didn't go but I watched the results in the angling Press the following week and I was sick to see that the lads who had gone over were getting 80 and 90 lb catches of roach.

I was sick at heart and felt that I should have been there with them. It was made even worse when the lads I knew personally came back and said what a great time they had enjoyed. The following year I went on the Benson and Hedges, it was the first

You don't have to be the tidiest angler to be the best. Ian in action on the River Blackwater in Ireland where he won his section in a Germany/Holland/England/Ireland International

visit I had made to Northern Ireland – and I came home with first prize and a new World match catch record!

It was the best fishing trip I had ever made.

Now of course I am invited to travel all over the country to do forums, teach-ins and films, and recently one of these took me over to Germany to see some of the British Army lads there. The main reasons were to attend their annual presentation and give them a talk-in on pole fishing – because the local Germans were giving our lads a bit of a hiding on this method.

The local river was called the Spree, and the day after the talk they took me down to the water and what an experience that was. To start with I fished it with a rod and reel because it looked so much like the river Trent. With a heavy balsa float in about ten feet of fairly fast flowing water I caught bream around the pound mark, but they were a different type of bream than we normally catch in England.

The fish were yellow, narrow and not as deep as our own specimens. I think they must have been built that way to combat the heavy flow of the river, but one thing was for certain . . . they still loved groundbait. Now whilst I was catching steadily on this balsa float I felt that there were a lot more fish there just waiting to be caught and as it turned out the method was to fish it with a pole and a hugh olivette lead.

At the time of writing you can't buy leads that big in this country, although I believe it is only a matter of time before they come over from Germany along with the big polystyrene-type floats which are used with them over there. These leads are equivalent to about five of our own swan shot.

I used one of these leads about nine inches from the hook with a tell-tale number four shot between it and the hook which was a forged 16 carrying two or three maggots. All of this was with the pole of course, and the method was to cast the lead upstream so that by the time it got to the bottom the float and the rest of your tackle was right in front of you. If you had cast in as normal your float would have run after your lead and by the time everything had settled it would have been time to come out for another.

With this method I was able to ease my tackle along with the flow which meant my bait was going along the river bed at a nice rate. This is important in all moving water – as I will explain elsewhere. Anyway, by inching the bait along I was able to get very

Private John Aitken travelled 400 miles to watch Ian during the 1977 World Championships in Luxemburg

positive bites and I was virtually catching a fish a cast which helped us put together some really big weights.

It was a different type of fishing than I had ever had before, and, to give you some idea of the heavy flow and quantity of fish, let me tell you about the bait needed during an average five-hour session. I was going through about 28 lb of dry groundbait and only three pints of maggots. That bread feed was all important. You had to mix it like concrete bricks to get it down and throw it in around a yard upstream so that it settled just in front of you.

I fed a ball of this groundbait (about the size of a tangerine) every single cast in and all of the Army lads really took to this method. They took it in turn to have a go on the pole and realised the great potential that was there. They had learnt exactly where they had gone wrong and since then they have had a fair amount of success.

In fact, this point was proved the very next day in a competition they organised and invited me to fish. I didn't win the event – I came second – and that was proof enough for me that the trip was well worth while.

8
My favourite river

The river Trent is one of the most popular, if not the most popular, water in the country. It has been the same story about the river ever since I was about 18 years old though. Many people fish it and end up going home heartbroken. They think they have done everything right and yet have only a few pounds of fish to show — whilst the angler at the next peg has had a sackful.

There was always a certain band of people who used to enjoy all of the success on the Trent and today it is very much the same with a certain number of regulars appearing in match results week in and week out. There were always a lot of people who nearly made it, a lot who couldn't fathom it out and a lot who used to go home heartbroken.

There was a method though, and that was slowing the bait down. Now just before I started fishing the Trent, maggot had been the number one bait on the river. But then the Manchester lads, myself included, were going down to the river and cleaning up on the caster. The big difference was that the caster needed fishing in a very different way to the maggot and, in fact, I didn't then know how to fish the maggot correctly.

Now to see what I mean you have to understand that the caster is a completely different bait to a maggot. It sinks much faster and behaves differently on the bottom. It tends to lie there and stick in one place or just move very slowly along the bottom.

A lot of people don't understand about the baits on the bottom. For example, when you look at a river and see the top moving at about ten miles per hour don't ever think that the speed at the bottom is anywhere near that. A little bit of thought, a little bit of commonsense will tell you that the speed at the bottom has got to be slower.

Ian carefully unhooks a roach

Ian wins his section on the Trent at Winthorpe with this net of fish

Imagine a rock on the river bottom with the water hitting it. Behind that rock there will be an eddy. The bottom third of the water will therefore be moving differently to the top two-thirds.

The way to fish this swim perfectly would be with a float as long as those top two-thirds. In around six feet of water that float would have to be four feet long, and anyone can tell you that this is not practicable.

With this in mind, you can then start to think how to set up your shotting patterns. Obviously you want to get your bait into that bottom half relatively fast when fishing the caster and you want to be able to hold back your float on the top so that the bait is acting as naturally as possible in that slower piece of water underneath, the piece where your bait is likely to be doing the most damage.

Now with regard to this slowing down of a bait I think it is best if I explain it with an actual instance of fishing which happened when I took a young lad, the son of a famous angler, to my local river, the Ribble, in Lancashire.

This lad had spent most of his time with his Dad, but he had spent it on Fenland waters where he was used to throwing out a waggler to beyond his feed, putting his rod tip under the water and then reeling in to sink his line so that his float was left there unhindered by conditions on the surface. This was all very well on these waters which have very little flow. But, on the Ribble, which is a faster moving water, it was totally wrong, especially in the type of swim that we were fishing. To start with, the flow on the inside was far faster than in the middle of the river and it was in the middle that I knew the chub, which we were after, lived. You can straightaway realise that by fishing a waggler and then sinking your line you are putting your line into a far faster flow than where your float was. This means your float is dragged along and off your feed. More important, it is dragged off its natural path.

I never said anything to the lad to start with, I just got on with my own fishing. I had put him downstream from me for a reason. It was a good peg, and I went in above (an equally good peg) but I also had a lot of casters which I fed heavy in order to pull fish into both of the pegs. I started to catch almost straightaway and after around two hours had about 20 lb in the net.

In this same period the young lad hadn't had a fish. I thought then that he had done enough his way for long enough and it was about time to show him the reason why he wasn't catching. I could see it was so easy and it was a chance to give him a lesson which I thought he would never forget.

The wind was right in favour of fishing with a double rubber float – upstream and at our back. I called the lad over and chucked out a double rubber float and told him to watch to see what I was doing. I laid the line on the water behind the float and, because of that wind, it was dead easy to do. When the float reached the end of the swim I went to mend the line but needn't have bothered as it was lying completely straight.

Now it got right to the end of the swim without a fish and, luckily, I was able to repeat this half a dozen times. It even had me fooled when it looked as though it would have gone under signalling a bite. But, if I had caught, it would have been an idiot fish.

The next cast I said to the youngster that we would do it differently and that we would catch a fish. The secret – and remember what I was saying about slowing that bait down – was that as soon as that float hit the river, instead of laying the line down, you had to stick the rod right up high in the air and hold every inch of line from the rod top to the float out of the water.

That upstream wind created a bow in the line, almost like a yacht sail, and by holding the rod just a fraction higher that float stood still in the middle of the river. As you lowered the rod gently, letting the air out of the sail as it were, then that float moved gently down the middle of the river. Gently, just lifting the rod again, I was able to hold it still again.

After the float had gone just a short distance at this slowed down rate under it went and I had a chub around the 1½ lb mark. The very next cast with the same method produced another chub. It was that simple. There were a million chub there but they wanted the bait putting to them right.

The lad quickly understood what was going on, went back to his peg, and then finished the day with about 25 lb of chub. He will never forget that day and it was a good lesson to learn – that the speed of the river is often, but not always, slower than on the top. There are days when this doesn't matter – and that is when you can catch these fish on the waggler running through at any rate. But when they need catching this method is the difference between your big weights and your little weights.

This, basically, was the secret not just for the Trent but for all moving water, especially with the caster. These days though there has been a big change from the caster to the maggot. Let's go back to the Trent specifically now and look at the difference.

The river has been cleaned up to such an extent that, in my opinion, it is overcleaned and now runs gin clear. There is a lot of weed growth in it and, because it is so clear, the fish will just not accept the caster as freely. You will catch fish on the caster, but, in the last decade, the maggot has taken over.

Let's have another look at one of the possible reasons behind this. The caster is a bait that must be fresh. I like to run them off the maggots one day and use them the next, I would never, ever dream of using them after three days. But, as more people got onto the bandwagon of using the caster, I believe bait was kept for a week and in some cases even a fortnight. By that time it was obviously stale.

I believe that the fish just got sick and tired of eating a stale bait and in fact it is just like us eating a stale nut. If you crack one open and it is stale you will try another but, if you get a couple of bad ones in a row, you will throw the whole bag away and eat something else. The nicer they are though the more you will eat.

The same thing applies with the caster and the fish. With a maggot they can practically guarantee that it is going to be good to eat. This, in my opinion, is one of the reasons for the big switch back to the maggot as the number one bait.

There is a big difference between fishing the caster and the maggot. In fact, the shotting patterns I have just discussed for the caster will not work – except in some cases – with the maggot. There are two main reasons for this; one is that the feeding pattern of the fish has changed in that they don't feed on the bottom as much, and the other is due to the way a maggot falls through the water. It weighs far less than a caster and therefore sinks to the bottom much slower. A maggot seems to hang in the water, especially when it gets to the area two feet off the bottom – it seems to travel twice as far as a caster before it comes to a rest, if indeed it stops at all. Provided the maggot is fed right (that is a little but all of the time) fish tend to rise up in the water to take the maggot – and for that reason it doesn't have to be fished on the bottom.

Therefore, the shotting patterns must be changed completely. We are talking now in terms of very light shotting patterns with the first shot being perhaps as far away as two foot from the hook.

Ian fishing overdepth at Crankley Point on the Trent

This allows a free-fall of the bait so that it looks more natural and means that the waggler will also work a lot more freely than it would with the caster. To fish the caster properly on a waggler we had to slow the bait down and the only way to do this efficiently was to keep adding depth, in some cases fishing as much as four feet overdepth on a clean bottom so that the bait was slowed down enough.

The opposite now works with the maggot. What you do, instead of going deeper and deeper and deeper to slow the bait down you keep going shallower because the fish are rising up to the loose feed and you want your hook bait running through with it. You can still slow your maggot down and catch, but not as much as you would with the caster when you were bottom fishing it.

Let's face it, fishing a river with a waggler is the easiest method there is. There is a lot more skill required in fishing a stick float. Providing that the waggler stays on course and your feeding pattern is right you will catch fish.

9
Learning from others

The finest way to learn your fishing is to watch others. Even though I served my time on the canals and then drifted away on to rivers and lakes because sport was better, I started to go back to my old haunts. To illustrate my point about learning, we have got to look at the big Greenall Whitley match on the Warrington Canal and the build up to it.

The week before I went to fish a match on the venue I was lucky to have Bobby Watson from Salford a few pegs away from me on one side and the great Benny Ashurst, father of my England team colleague Kevin Ashurst, a few pegs away on the other side. I had about $2\frac{1}{2}$ lb of fish in this match. Benny had slightly more than me and Bobby topped 3 lb, if I remember correctly.

I went to watch Bobby fishing and saw that he had a dumpy float on with no shot on the bottom. He was fishing tight up against the far bank. When I went to watch Benny I noticed his tackle was almost the opposite, despite the fact he was also fishing that far bank.

Benny had shot on the bottom and he had a thin topped float on. As I watched I could see the reasons why they were both fishing differently, even though they were both fishing over the canal and lying their line on the bottom, giving the fish a still bait.

Now, I liked Benny's float best but fancied Bobby's shotting pattern. That helped me make my decision on how to tackle up. The other thing I learnt during the match. Everyone else was fishing the other bank, but I thought I would have a go under my rod end for a short spell just in the boat run.

I got five bites on the caster fishing this line. Using this bait on this venue means that when you get a bite it is usually from a decent roach, usually of a 6 oz minimum but quite often of 10 to

47

14 oz class. I missed every one of those bites, but thought to myself that if I had been using a pole at the time I would have hooked those fish.

With this information at the back of my mind I went up to the canal for a practice session during the week and got a mate of mine to fish the pole. In fact I told him a bit of a lie because I said they had been slaughtering the fish on the pole under the rod end. Really, I only wanted to use him to see what the potential was. Meanwhile, I was going to play around with this method of fishing the far bank.

So with a thin topped float and no shot on the bottom I started fishing – and ended up with 20 lb of roach on every peg I tried. I had never done that on a canal before. The weight had come from a good area, but the other thing was that this mate of mine on the pole also had four sets of double figures.

These were two lots of outstanding weights from a canal where normally 7 lb is a good weight, even pleasure fishing, from the far side.

I drew my peg for the competition and was immediately told that a match hadn't been won there for years. When I found out how deep it was across, my heart sunk. It was just ten inches. Nevertheless, despite the fact I was hoping for 18 inches, I tackled up to fish about 18 inches overdepth without a shot on the bottom and a No. 8 just off under a thin peacock waggler.

By casting right across I managed to get that small shot just resting on the bottom and that float showing a good quarter of an inch. Then, by pulling the float about ten inches from the far bank and into the deeper water I lifted the No. 8 off the bottom and the float would sink accordingly. I fed six casters regularly right over and six under the rod end for the boat run swim.

I sat and waited for 20 minutes before the first bite. It took the float away nice and smoothly and striking very carefully and lifting the rod I was able to lead the fish away like a little dog on a lead so that it didn't splash about and scare anything else that might be in the swim. That fish went 10 oz.

Immediately, I cast back in and took another roach. Now I knew the fish had arrived but instead of making the third cast and taking a fish, as I know I should have done, I just fed. I picked up the pole and came close in. What I was doing was resting those fish on the far line, giving them feed steadily so that they would stay there and become really confident. All that was needed was those six casters now and again.

Meanwhile, because it was the first time I had gone on the pole in that match, despite the fact that I had been feeding the swim steadily, my first cast produced a nice slide away bite and a hybrid about 8 oz which was quickly followed by another. I went back on to the rod on the far swim and took two more fish. Then a boat came and he thought he was doing everyone a favour when he went to the far bank of the canal.

That disturbed the fish, but by then I was ready to come back to the pole again and leave that far swim. As the match went on I kept the same pattern, feeding both swims all the time but swapping between the pole and the rod and line. This helped me to keep in contact and finish with 20 fish for 7 lb 3oz – and another £800 in the bank.

One thing that happened in this match, sponsored by a brewery, made me laugh because it happens so often now. Different

Ian attracts a crowd wherever he fishes nowadays

pubs and clubs got invitations and a lot of families, wives and kids, turn up for the day out.

Now a lot of people ask me how my fishing is going, and I have got to answer that I am on a hiding to nothing every time I go out. If I win a match everyone expects it, because they say I am the former World Champion. If I don't win or if I get beaten either side of me they ask: 'How could he ever become World Champion?'

On this particular day one of the things that really pleased me was a woman who came up to me after the draw. I had heard her talking to her husband as we crossed the field to the canal and he told her who I was and that I had just won the World Championship. She came over and asked me if I was Ian Heaps and if I was going to win. She meant it in all sincerity because she thought I had the ability to win if I wanted. When I did win it meant a lot more to me because of her question.

10
The England Manager

Stan Smith, the England team manager, has been heavily criticised from a number of sources for a variety of reasons, including who he has and has not selected, and the teams' performances in the World matches. Well, I have known Stan since early 1975 and, as a member of his team, I would like to put forward some views which have not been put forward before.

Let's start when I first met Stan, when he selected me for my first England match. I was really glad to get my chance and was very grateful for it, whoever the rest of the team were wasn't of any concern to me. Over the years I have realised the amount of effort which this man puts in for England. His sole ambition is to see England take away that World team title and I just hope I am there to see his face when he realises he has finally done it.

I know he comes in for a lot of criticism, but a lot of the people who criticise the man haven't got a clue to what goes on in the background. I didn't, when I was first picked, but I am now involved in organising matches myself and I realise the amount of work that takes place. When you think Stan is doing this on a much more important scale with the World Championships, the importance of it all is incredible.

The amount of effort which Stan Smith puts into this is absolutely incredible; in fact it is a lifetime's work. I totally admire him for his persistence in spite of all the criticism, because a lesser man would have said 'to hell with the lot of you' and told people to get a new boss. Without a doubt we are in a good position, having such a strong-willed man.

Give the Continentals an inch and they will take a mile, but Stan, who has dealt with these people for such a long time, knows just how to keep them under a tight reign and they respect him

Stan Smith at the head of the team before the 1976 World Championships in Bulgaria

THE ENGLAND MANAGER

for it. No way will his team get shoved to one side or pushed into a corner. There is no way they will be trodden on whilst he is the manager because other officials, who have been around the same length of time as him, know they cannot mess him or his boys about.

That alone is a good thing – to know that your manager is in such a respected position and right behind you. No matter what team he has picked Stan has been behind them a hundred per cent. If he has picked you no-one can say a word against you – unless they come up with something that is true when Stan will investigate.

As an example of his devotion in time alone – never mind the expense – immediately after his return from the World Championship in Spain he booked a ticket and was off to Germany to look at the next venue. It is a non-stop job and time, effort and everything else concerned is nothing to him. He is a man of steel and does a marvellous job.

A lot of people think the England Team have a great time. You

The 1976 England team in Bulgaria. Left to right: (back) Stan Smith, Mark Downes, Tony Scott, Ken Giles; (front) Kevin Ashurst, Ivan Marks and Ian

know, they're off to Spain again to lounge in the sun and live it up. These people don't know the half of it. We average four hours sleep a day whilst we are on the World match. For example, when we went to Spain I was up at 4 a.m. to drive down to Heathrow airport – a journey of around 250 miles – with Kevin Ashurst so that we could link up with the rest of the team. There were flight delays and numerous other problems which meant it took us 24 hours to get to our hotel.

We were in bed for just two hours, then we were up again and off to the practice session. From practice we had to go to the official parade, back to the hotel for a 10.30 p.m. dinner and the problems of sorting out bait and tackle for the next day. Don't forget the team meeting before we went to bed as well! The following morning it was up at 5.30 a.m. in order to get to the match then after the event the official reception and another late night. Then up early again on the last day to get the coach and plane home.

You virtually go without sleep. It is not a holiday, it is hard work. The first time you go through it you are on fire, bubbling with enthusiasm but worrying and wondering if you are going to do your best, hoping that you won't let the rest of the team down. What made it worse for me was the huge crowd there – 30,000 plus – and they were all standing on the opposite bank, a real frightening mob. I regard myself as unflappable, things don't bother me, but these crowds make you wonder and you know you daren't make a mistake. As it turned out it was an easy debut for me once I had landed the first of the big fish. From then on the crowd was on my side and willing me on to win.

At first, you begin to think about what you are doing when crowds are around. You make sure that everything is right and you try to fish better. Now I just get on with it and don't think about the crowds any more. You blank them out of your mind but now and again – probably as you net a good fish – you get a clap or a cheer, a nice reminder that they are still there.

11
Sponsored matches

There appears to be an increasing trend towards big-name sponsored matches. Events like the Ladbroke, Colt 45, Gladding Masters and other matches which offer big prize money and give the ordinary angler the chance to see the country's big names in action at the same time and place.

I think – and hope – that these type of events will continue to grow. They have already proved how popular they are by drawing in crowds which are the equivalent to those at football matches in the Third and Fourth Divisions. Considering that angling is not always the best of sports to watch, it is much more of a participant game, this must show a greal deal of interest. Not only that, it also helps anglers learn a lot about different methods.

The finest way to learn about angling is not just to sit and read books but to spend time on the bank watching people. As I did in my younger days, don't watch and copy, watch and understand and put your own thoughts to whatever you see. With all these sponsored matches, it gives anyone who is interested a chance to watch people who have got something special, and to see just what it is so that they, the spectators, can capitalise on it.

You will never be better than a man by copying him. But, if you understand what he is doing it is easy to learn and develop your own methods from there. I watched two top-class anglers on the Trent one day after I had drawn a grueller of a peg which gave me no chance of even getting into the frame. They were next to each other but only one was slaughtering the fish. To anyone watching it must have been as obvious why one was catching and the other wasn't.

They were both using maggots and at the end of the day they said that they had used about six pints of feed. They had fished

Steve Gardener, one of the South's top anglers, nets a bream. Note how his tackle is all to hand with his bait, catapult, keepnet and groundbait just beside him. All this leads to a better angler

SPONSORED MATCHES

almost identical rigs, yet one man had 22 lb and the other had 4 lb. After watching them for ten minutes the reason why one was catching more than the other was staring you right in the eye. All it was, was that one bloke was feeding two or three times every cast in, giving him a constant flow of maggots going through his swim but the other man didn't feed for two casts, and then when he did

Ian puts another Trent chub safely into the net

he put a great big handful in. It was easy to see that the fish were following the steady stream of food to them.

There are so many things in angling which are obvious that just by studying anglers in action you can learn – even if it is sometimes by their mistakes.

The standard of match fishing is improving drastically every year. It is getting to the stage now where you are getting a hard nucleus of match anglers throughout the country and no matter where you fish you seem to know almost every one of them individually. Those people who seem to have been left behind appear to have given up the game or gone back to club matches.

Why is it then, that the same anglers come up regularly? I think it is about a state of mind, just like any other sport. It is so important that you have the will to win, the killer instinct. I have always had that, but now it is more important to me because I have to think of my reputation.

There is only going to be one time when I will pack in match fishing – when I am in a box! I just hope that I am fit enough when I get older so that I can walk the banks with my tackle. I have never thought about what would happen if I stopped winning, I want to think that it will never happen.

I think Benny Ashurst is the best example of what every true match angler wants to be. As 65 he is still walking the banks in all conditions and maintaining his great record. He still travels to the Trent to take on some of the best in the country and is out in weather which would kill other men of his age – never mind all the standing he has to do during a match.

There is one great thing that keeps Benny at the top, and others like him. Dedication and understanding. He is quick to learn and has the ability to watch and pick up information. Also, you will find that all the top anglers have incredible memories. They can go back 20 years and tell you not only where a match was won but also the method that was used. The information is always there, logged away, and I think their minds play a great part in how they fish each day though they may not actually realise it.

Some people are natural anglers, they have it born in them, whilst others have to work really hard to achieve success. Quite often on my first visit to waters I end up winning. I have the ability to read a water – though of course I do sometimes make mistakes – but I normally have a rough idea of what is required on the day.

Benny Ashurst, one of the greatest anglers England has ever produced

Sometimes that is not only governed by such things as the flow, floods and weather.

A lot of people try to read far too much into their fishing. They try to become far too scientific when you must keep it as simple as possible: fish as efficiently as you can. Say I went to the Trent and heard the winning method was loose feeding and fishing 40 yards out with a float, there is no way I am going to attempt that if the wind is blowing right into my face. I wouldn't be able to feed or fish the line correctly under those conditions. Some people will say why don't you cast a swimfeeder out to where the fish were caught before? Well, that is not the point. You must adapt to the conditions, even if that means fishing three rod lengths out instead of five. You must fish to the best of your ability and use the method which is most comfortable.

12
Swimfeeder

One of the upsetting things of recent years has been the general trend towards the swimfeeder. It has happened, I think, because of the tremendous barbel explosion on the River Severn and the massive head of big fish like bream, carp and especially chub on the River Trent. It is upsetting for a top class float fisherman who has served a hard apprenticeship.

It is disappointing to think anyone can come along with the feeder and score; after all, a bad cast with a swimfeeder is still a good one because his groundbait is right there, next to his hookbait. Obviously though, anyone who can put that feeder in the same place regularly still stands a better chance.

Don't get me wrong though – I am not against swimfeeders. If it is good for angling and fishing, let people use the swimfeeder, even though I do not like to use it. I don't like seeing it in use, but I would never think of banning it because it gives so many people so much enjoyment.

Fishing is a science, as I describe elsewhere in this book when I deal with floats, and it is just the same with fishing the swimfeeder; there is a right and a wrong way. The more people use these feeders the more educated they become. It is not just a matter of casting a swimfeeder into the same spot every time – although that is important – it is knowing where to cast it.

The place to cast it for the best results is directly in front of you. It is a matter of balanced tackle. A lot of people will think I am talking a lot of eyewash when I talk of swimfeeders and balanced tackle, but they would be wrong.

If, when you cast that feeder in front of you it does not hold bottom, reel in and keep adding lead until it will hold. Don't just use the feeder with the lead it holds when you buy it. Carry around some lead strips in your tackle box to add onto it. The less lead you can use, the better balanced the tackle will be. If it is also possible to hold your rod high in the air I advise you to do so. This will also lead to you using less lead on your feeder than you would need if it was on the rod rest. This is because there is not so much line in the water for the current to catch and pull out of position.

This means that you can fish a lot further out and use a lot less lead. It also means a better tackle balance and it could also help you out on the strike, leading to a better hook hold on the fish and possibly less fish 'bumped' off the hook as you strike.

Now between your rod tip – which will have a quivertip to register bites – there will be a bow to the feeder. When a fish takes the bait it will probably dislodge the feeder which, because of its finely balanced position with the amount of lead it is carrying, will give you the bite. But this bite is not the normal pull you would expect on your rod tip. As the fish is releasing all the pressures on the rod top, more often than not the tip will spring back and then pull over. If you strike when the tip falls back you will still find in most cases that the fish are on the hook.

Just like float fishing, it is important to keep refilling the feeder with bait. A lot of people ask me what is the best shotting pattern for the Trent and my reply to them is that before they start worrying about where to put their shot they should get their feeding patterns right. You must learn to feed on a regular basis so that the fish are charged up, and they get to know exactly when the next amount of food, is going to arrive.

Once you get those fish waiting for that next helping of feed – which is usually every cast on the float – you should be able to catch them. You can't catch the fish when they aren't there. So, especially on a river which is flowing, the most important thing is to get a feeding pattern going. Then, there are a thousand and one shotting patterns which will catch them.

Obviously, this means that every cast with the swimfeeder you should be putting in more bait. The question you are all asking now is when to bring in the feeder? Well, my answer is to bring it out as soon as you think the bait has gone. Perhaps it might be worth leaving it in for an extra few seconds, but if there are plenty of fish about you want the feed to empty out even faster. To do this, a good gimmick is to make slits between the holes on the feeder so the maggots or casters get out just that bit quicker.

SWIMFEEDER

There are two main sorts of feeders, the block end and the open ended ones which you use groundbait in. A lot depends on where you are fishing on which ones to use. If I am fishing a place where I think the fish will accept minimum amounts of groundbait I would use the open feeder with maggots inside and just block the end with the groundbait.

There are a lot of places where groundbait has the same effect as cyanide and these are where the block end feeder comes into its own. Just the same, if I thought there were a few bream about – and groundbait generally makes this species feed – I would like to have a bit of groundbait going in with the casters and maggots.

The feeder would be attached to the main line by short link of line about four or five inches long. My hook would be attached by another piece of line to this rig and would vary from one foot to a yard, depending on how the fish are feeding. Generally speaking the shyer the fish are, the longer the distance between the main line and hook must be. This is something which you just cannot tell anyone, you must experiment on the day to find out what is best.

Sometimes, you will be fishing a very long tail and getting small bites which you can't hit or don't even see and you might find that a shorter hook length will bring better results. Sometimes on this short tail the bites are so good that the rod is almost pulled off the rest because the fish are practically hooking themselves.

Sizes of hooks and line obviously vary, but generally I would say that the main line from your reel has got to be around the 6 lb mark. This is because when you are fishing and casting the feeder out all the time you are putting the line under a lot of stress. After five hours fishing you will probably find the line will want renewing anyway. Normally my link to the feeder will also be 6 lb, and, if I can get away with it, I like to use a 3 lb hook length. There will still be times though when you will have to go down to fine lines and small hooks just to get the fish tricked into biting.

I have watched fish feeding in clear water on maggots thrown in by hand but if you put a maggot through with a tiny No. 20 hook on a 1 lb or $1\frac{1}{2}$ lb line they will just totally ignore it. In fact, I used to go on holiday to a place in Northern Scotland and fish on a tidal river which was full of sea trout (they are called finnock in the area) about the 1 lb mark. This isn't going to go down well with the gamefishers, but I used to go up there with a gallon of maggots and float fish for them.

It wasn't worth considering fishing a hook smaller than a No. 12, but it used to be frustrating to watch these fish gobble up every maggot thrown in by hand and yet see them not even look at the ones with a hook in them. It would take ten or twelve offers by a fish before the idiot of the shoal actually got your bait into its mouth. At times you could see the fish dart towards your bait and then, at the last minute, turn away.

13
How to use groundbait

Groundbait and when to use it is something that baffles a lot of people. Many are frightened to use it in the quantities that they should, whilst others just over feed the fish by piling it into the water. Others are puzzled about what the conditions should be like when they put it in.

One of the waters that I fish is very clear and the type of place where many anglers would be scared stiff of putting in groundbait What I use here is black peat – and it could be that it would be the answer for you when fishing in one of your own gin clear waters proves very difficult.

What the groundbait contains is black peat – or what I call a Continental mix which has a few grains of ordinary groundbait added. The mix is dampened so that when it is thrown in, it gives a suspension in the water. This creates cover for the fish and the idea is to keep feeding it continuously so that there is a nice cloud in the water. Your hand should never be out of the groundbait container. Fish not only shelter in this cloud but they also recognise it as a feeding area and, if you add a few bloodworm or jokers, you will find the perch especially have the confidence to feed readily.

I have had a lot of success over the years fishing bloodworm with this cloud, and one of the amazing things is the depth at which you can catch fish whilst the water is warm. You can catch them at a foot or six inches below the surface.

On one occasion I had a two hour evening match on a lake and I had perch coming at the rate of one a cast. I had a very bad last 15 minutes in which I took only six fish. A friend of mine, a non-angler, was sitting besides me and he was quite enthralled by it all. He had never caught a fish in his life. I was fishing with a small

Ian holding several 'cannonballs' of feed . . .

HOW TO USE GROUNDBAIT

pole float and small weight just six inches from the hook. The fish were taking at about 18 inches, in about four or five feet of water.

They were coming up into a suspended black cloud and picking out the food which was in it. I ended up winning the match with 3 lb 2 oz, and after I had weighed-in my friend asked if he could have a go. On his first cast he hooked a fish which came off. Because he was so inexperienced the tackle just shot up into the air and ended up in a tangle the like of which you have never seen.

I tried to untangle it but failed, so his float ended up six inches from the hook. That big tangle was between the two! Jokingly, I baited up the hook and told him that if the fish were there he

... and using them to bait his swim ready for the 1977 World Championships in Luxemburg

would get one. Well, would you believe that as fast as he put in he was getting a fish, and he turned to me and said: 'It's easy this fishing lark.' Those fish were just six inches below the surface and how we never saw them I can't understand.

The nice thing about this method is that you can also bring the fish right close in and catch them practically at your feet.

Now if I was fishing a river I would look for a bit of colour in the water before using groundbait. I am usually against using groundbait when the water is clear, as I have had so many failures with it. But when there is a hint of colour you can get away with the groundbait. It can be fairly heavy – although there are times when you have to mix it so that it breaks on impact.

Let's say that winter is when you want the groundbait to get right down on the bottom. You must mix it heavy so that it sinks right in front of you and gets to work. In the summer though, cloud is the answer as fish tend to feed in mid-water which is warmer. Roach tend to be the best mid-water feeders with bream towards the bottom. Now, obviously, even if you use cloud bait some of it is going to get on the bottom and every now and then it is going to pay off if you put extra depth onto your tackle and see if those bream or bigger fish are on the bottom.

One thing I find about groundbaiting, whether you are going to put it in as cloud or heavy, is that once you have decided you are going to use it don't use it half-heartedly. If you do only half use it it seems to have the effect of scaring the fish. If you put a ball in initially and then wait another 20 minutes before putting in any more it can frighten them, but if you keep putting it in they get used to it. If you can get the fish onto the groundbait it is by far the best way of getting fish.

Once you get fish coming to groundbait it is very easy to concentrate your feed and you get the fish in a small area.

Shallow swims often put people off groundbaiting, whether it is on a river or pond. On the Ribble, which I fish a lot, there are numerous dace, which frequent the shallower spots in the summer and which love groundbait. There are times there when I have been catching steadily by just loose feeding maggots but when I have decided to put groundbait in I found the fish came straight onto it and fed ravenously. Instead of having to trot down the swim to the fish they have come to me.

This is just another effect of groundbait. It can bring fish right

Ian keeps an eye on the scales as his 1977 World catch is weighed

up the river, right under your rod top at times. When the fish do this and really want the food you must use the groundbait freely. Quite often when it is like this the fish will regurgitate the groundbait as you are unhooking them and you won't be able to see your hook.

A lot of the waters we fish on the World Championship respond well to heavy groundbaiting and, a fortnight before we go on the match, I quite often go to Compstall Reservoir to practise throwing groundbait about 30 yards. I am not there to catch fish, just to get my arm into the right action. I will still bait up my hook though, and cast properly as if I am fishing.

But, even during these practice sessions, the things I have learned on this difficult-to-fish water are amazing. I was there one time and had literally thrown a heap of bait at the fish – really it was all just a waste – but when I reeled in I discovered I had had a bite. I threw the next ball of bait in, cast, and then decided to wait a few minutes instead of bringing straight out. I caught straightaway and realised that because of this constant stream of feed the fish had moved in.

The groundbait had been mixed fairly heavy so that it would break into a cloud only after it had sunk a couple of feet in the water. The only reason these fish really came to it, I reckon, is because it was going in all the time. This is a point which I think is more worth remembering than the fact that you must use it heavier in faster flowing water. If you are going to use groundbait then use it! It doesn't always matter if the fish are eating it or not – they will recognise it as a carrier of food and move into your swim.

14
Pole fishing

Pole fishing is something which, I am glad to say, has caught on in this country over the past few years. It is good really because it will help us to compete more efficiently at World level. There is no doubt that the Continentals have beaten us hands down over the years because of their mastery of the pole, but now our knowledge of it is improving fast.

Already, I believe that we know more about using the pole than they do about using our rods and reels. They are keen to learn about our methods though, so we must master the pole as fast as we can to ensure that we can become the best all-rounders in the World.

Basically, the big advantage of the pole is bait presentation. You can put a bait more accurately into one spot with a pole than any other means and make it work just how you want it to. Now the ideal method of using the pole is with a minimum amount of line between the end of the pole and the float. This would mean about two feet between the float and the pole tip, giving you around eight feet of line in six feet of water

This control is especially important when you are fishing with the bloodworm and I have done a lot of experiments with them and jokers in a goldfish tank to prove my point. This has helped me to understand why the Continentals use this short line method and has led to our own team adopting it in recent World matches.

You can try the experiment yourself. Throw a pinch full of jokers (that's about a dozen) into a gold fish tank and watch how they wriggle in a figure of eight formation right to the bottom. The goldfish come along to investigate and see these things wriggling like mad on the bottom of the tank and they can't resist them. What I have noticed is that these fish stand on their heads and eat three worms one at a time before levelling off on their bellies to chew and digest this mouthful of food.

Then, they will stand on their heads again and go through the same motions. The only exception to the rules is when these jokers do what I call their 'dance'. This is when they suddenly rise up from the bottom to the surface and then drop back down. I noticed that very rarely did these jokers get up more than three inches because the fish found them so irresistable that they snapped them up, even if they had a mouthful of food already.

This brings us to the short line tactic. The way to tackle up is with a float with an olivette lead, to take the bait straight to the bottom, and a small shot just below that to drop the bait slowly for the last few inches. When the bait gets down bites are usually instant when you are using bloodworm, but if you don't get a bite as soon as it has settled just lift that float out of the water with the pole, thus repeating the joker's dance: this will almost certainly produce a bite if the fish are there.

That method is something which you would not be able to do with a rod and line across a canal, or eight metres out in a pond where you have to fish a little waggler. The difference between a man working his bait like this or just using the same tackle and waiting for a bite to come along is amazing. I reckon it could mean twice or even three times as much weight for the man prepared to work.

I first got involved with pole because of the World Championship matches and by watching the Continentals in practice the day before the main match. I thought it was an interesting way of fishing, especially when I saw the results, but the main thing which spurred me on in pole fishing was when we fished the World match in Luxemburg.

This was a river very much like the Trent which had been so good to me for a number of years. When the English team arrived very early in the morning for a practice session there wasn't a soul in sight and there was a bit of a mist on the water – but there were good quality roach rising everywhere.

The England team manager, Stan Smith, instead of putting us in a set order on the bank so that we could compete against each other as usual, let us sit anywhere because he could see the enthusiasm of the team and just how many fish there were to be

POLE FISHING

caught. He gave us three hours to do what we liked.

The similarities to the Trent were amazing. There were stone banks and we all rushed down to the river. I put on a fairly heavy stick float like most of the others, but they were soon on to a balsa; then some changed to a waggler and I changed to a slider to see if I could catch like that. But we caught hardly anything between us. It was unbelievable, because it was a river full of fish – we had seen them – yet at the end of three hours the six of us only caught about 20 fish.

As excited as we were when we first arrived, it had soon been knocked out of us by this result. The next practice session we took along bloodworm and caught one or two more fish, but nothing like what we had heard the river was capable of.

But when a team from the home country came along – 100 yards from us – and started to practise, we noticed them catching steadily. I took a walk along the bank to investigate and found them all on heavy floats with the short line approach on the pole. Now the important thing was that they put groundbait in heavy and swung the olivette weight on the lines upstream, so that by the time it settled it was just about to drift over that feed on the bottom.

They caught all of their fish in the next yard because they were able to hold their bait right over that false bed of bloodworms, jokers and feed they had put in. If they didn't get a bite they just lifted out and put the tackle back in upstream again. When those fish arrived on the feed it was virtually a fish every put in. Now that showed me a method of presentation which you just couldn't master on a rod and reel.

Watching them that day made me realise that back home there were a hundred and one places where this application could be used with success.

Now let's have a look at the business end of the tackle, which as you are now probably aware, centres mostly around the olivette, the pear shaped lead which is used to get the bait down fast. These leads come in a number of different sizes to match the floats and go up to quite a size.

But a recent visit to Germany revealed to me that there are some even bigger ones on the market which are the equivalent in weight to one of our own bombs which weigh around half an

73

ounce. These leads are used with polystyrene Avon type floats in around ten feet of strong-flowing river water. I have used these like the Germans do and found that I can catch 100 lb of bream in a day – or being more realistic around 40 1-lb bream in a five hour match. Yet in the same peg, using a rod and reel with three swan shot down on a heavy float, you just cannot get the same results. In fact, I started to catch roach on this German venue. For every ten fish you would catch four roach with the rod and line, yet on the pole you would get nine bream and just one roach because of the difference in presentation. Also, it took you a lot longer to catch those ten fish on the rod.

Obviously, you cannot always catch best with either bulk shot or an olivette down the line. So, when do you change to the more normal pattern of stringing out shot? Usually I would do this when I thought I could catch on the drop as the bait flutters through the water. There are times though, when other shotting patterns will score for you. I would change to these when conditions needed – just as I would with a rod and reel.

For instance, I have caught on the River Weaver in Cheshire with a method which also works on the pole. I used to fish overdepth and let the bait hang over the shelf with a strung out shotting pattern. By using this method on the pole I have found that, at times, it is more effective than the olivette – it is just a method that I like because it has caught for me throughout the years.

Usually though, I have found the method to work better on the pole because I am holding the tackle over the shelf which is just too far out for the rod and line to present the bait correctly. With the rod and reel it has meant going grossly overdepth to get the presentation right; but with the pole I can shorten off considerably which means the bait is presented the same but the bites register more quickly and are more positive.

Now there are three methods of pole fishing which all require different tops for your pole. There is the short line, which I have already mentioned which is for bait presentation; there is the long line when presentation doesn't mean a lot and bites are coming freely; and then there is method between them where there is a medium length of line out and it usually means unshipping a few sections so that you can swing the tackle to hand.

What type of tip you use on these three methods depends a lot

POLE FISHING

on what you are catching and what tackle you are using. Most poles nowadays come with a flick tip which is a soft action top used mostly for snatching out small fish. They are not used with the shock absorber elastic which is needed when you are using light line and small hooks and when you may expect to catch a big fish.

Most of the flick tips have eyes on them through which you can tie your line. However, I prefer to remove these eyes and fasten the line to the pole with two pieces of valve rubber. What I do is pass the line through the first piece of rubber and then push this a few inches along the tip. Then, the line is wrapped around the tip a few times in a coil fashion before the other valve rubber, which the line also passes through, is pushed onto the tip.

This may sound a bit of a fragile set up, but believe me it works and there is no need for knots or glue or anything else. The big advantage of this is that you can shorten the line off if necessary – and you do not keep shortening the tackles you may have made up by keeping on tying them to the tip and then having to snap them off every time you finish fishing.

The other most commonly used tip is fitted with a crook which is generally an alloy attachment glued onto the end of the pole. This bends down at right angles from the pole. It is fitted with a groove at the very end where a loop can be placed from the elastic shock absorber and then kept in there with a plastic sleeve which slides over the entrance.

I would normally use this set-up with light tackle where there are some good quality fish and where I could quite easily be caught out and smashed unless I had this safety precaution.

The first type of tip, the soft action one, is my favourite and I have modified a few of them so that I can fish elastic with them if necessary. To do this I fish with the elastic inside the tip. I have a number of tips made up ready for use, but with different strengths of elastic for different size fish and different size hooks and breaking strain lines.

Here is how they are modified. First, an eye of some kind, preferably the lining from the inside of a lined rod ring, should be glued into the end of the tip to prevent the elastic from fraying against the pole edge. Then, the elastic is run into the pole. At the other end of this tip section I have a hollow plastic tube which will just fit into the tip but which does not get into the way of the ferrules on the pole. The elastic is put into this tube and is stopped from being pulled out of it by a wedge of wood or something similar.

At the tip end the elastic is stopped from going inside of the pole by a small bead which is in turn stopped from falling off by a loop. The loop itself can be used to tie your main line onto.

The advantage of using the elastic is that you should not get caught out by the bigger fish. For example, the first big fish I landed with this elastic was a 3 lb chub from the River Ribble. When I hit it I did not know how big it was – all I could see was the rubber streaming out of the end of the pole. By just holding the pole motionless the fish came to the top and was beaten. Now the big secret is that when you are fishing a rod and reel and feel a good fish, you tend to give it line. By giving it line the fish feels it has a chance and the fight takes some time.

Now while the rubber stretches, it gets progressively stronger without any erractic paying out of line or stopping it, and as the fish dives to the bottom the rubber forces the fish to the top. I have caught carp to 5 lb on the rubber but lost bigger ones which just wouldn't stop and with which you have no chance anyway.

When you buy your first pole go for the longest one that is available. Don't make the mistake of buying a short one – too many people do because it suits their pocket at the time. Then they find that with an extra metre or two they can just reach over the shelf on a canal or river with the short line method. They see that with the extra distance they don't need to stretch their arms out at full length. This means it costs them twice as much because they have had to buy two poles instead of one.

How far out you fish with the pole is very important, especially with the bloodworm. With the worm it is important to plumb the depth very accurately so that the bait is in that magic spot at the bottom of a shelf. It is no use fishing bloodworm on a sloping shelf, you must keep searching for that level bottom. That is where you feed and that determines where you will fish and the length of pole needed. The ideal place to have your bait just half an inch off the bottom, just where the fish's mouth is when it is on its belly.

The next thing to look at is the rigidity. A good pole is a light one which is fairly rigid. The best in this field is obviously carbon fibre, but this is way out of the price range of many people and not exactly the best thing for a first-time pole angler to buy. It is no use having a pole which sways about and bends in the wind.

I would always go for the take apart poles as these are firmer. Also, look for the reverse ferrule types where the handle goes inside the next piece up and not the second piece inside the handle. Even better, look for the ones with the biggest ferrules. The longer they are the more rigid that pole is going to be.

Carbon fibre has been one of the biggest breakthroughs in angling for a number of years and has allowed manufacturers to build rods which are extremely light, a point which must be in their favour as on many occasions you will have to hold them all day long.

But, for me, the rods aren't right yet. The main thing I have against carbon rods is that once they are made up it feels nothing like the blank. Pick up the carbon blank and it feels just right, stiff with a nice tip action. But the trouble is that once you put rings on it the blank goes all floppy. It goes so soft that it is not the ideal weapon.

Once carbon is developed to the extent that it feels the same when it is finished as the blanks do now without the eyes whipped on, then I would say it is right. At that time, though, I can imagine people having trouble selling the product. Anglers will walk into a shop, pick up the rod and think it felt too much like a poker. In the shop it might feel that way, but on the bank I believe it will be right.

Carbon rods of today are the other way round. When you pick them up in the shop they feel right but, when you get them on the bank and hook a fish, you have an almost right through action. You really have to bend into a fish before you can make any impression on it and get it to the net. You don't even get the feeling of your fish properly. It is the same with any rod in my view; it should feel too stiff for the angler when he is in the shop.

Having said all that, I must admit that I do use a carbon rod. It is one which I put my name to but which is not on the market now. Also, it is a modified version. It is a very, very stiff rod. In fact, it used to be so stiff that it would easily kill big fish and made it easy work to get good quality fish in.

I took the top piece out and replaced part of it with a glass roach pole tip and in other words, I now have a very stiff rod with a top that is soft. It suits me down to the ground. People who see and try it fall in love with it straight away. It is a great rod which still

Ian in action with a carbon pole on Northern Ireland's River Bann at Portadown

retains its lightness, but if anyone can make something the same wholly in carbon I think it would be a super rod.

At the time of writing some people are going carbon fibre mad and even using carbon leger rods – to me it is pointless and a complete waste of money. When you are using float tackle and constantly have the rod in your hand carbon is great, but when you use a bomb rod where the rod is mostly on a rest it is stupid – if it goes much further some will even want carbon bank sticks!

Without a doubt one of the major breakthroughs with carbon has been the carbon fibre pole. Let's face it, carbon has allowed us to talk in terms of ten metre poles and the longer you can get a pole the better, because it helps bait presentation so much.

I can remember fishing the World Championship in Luxemburg and carbon poles weren't really 'in' in this country then – a lot of people were struggling with nine metre glass poles. I struggled in that match with the fibreglass pole and now, looking back I know life would have been a lot easier if I had possessed the two carbon poles I have now. The Continentals had the carbon poles that day and they found it very easy.

In the case of poles it is not just the extra lightness that is a benefit of carbon. They can also be made a lot thinner which makes them easier to hold, more rigid and means they are not affected as much by winds which tend to catch hold of glass ones and make them difficult to handle.

The price of £400 to £600 tends to put a lot of people off carbon poles, but I think that if you are a dedicated matchman they are a must. In my first year of pole fishing I won £900 plus which meant I not only paid for my pole but also made a profit – and the good thing is that I still have the pole. Without that pole I believe that I couldn't have won the matches that I did, I just couldn't have put the bait to the fish as they wanted it.

There's one angler in Lancashire, I've heard, who got a bank loan to get his pole and I think that's a good idea if you are keen enough and want to win. For example, if I were to blindfold you and take you to the Lancaster Canal today – providing no one spoke – I could tell you that you were in France and you couldn't call me a liar because ninety per cent of the people would be using the pole because they realise its potential on this type of hard-fished water.

15
Popular floats

There are so many different types and makes of floats on the market now that it is easy to see why many anglers are confused about which type they should use and when. Often, they will buy a float because it looks good. I know that many people will advise you about when to use different kinds of floats but let me give you a piece of advice: after considering what float you should use on a certain occasion, according to what you have been told, consider whether you think it will do the job you want it to.

For instance, the waggler, or float which is attached to your line only by its bottom end, is generally used when you are fishing more than two lengths out. There are occasions, though, when you could use it to great advantage just under your rod top. So, the message is that you should not be hard and fast in your ways. Be prepared to experiment. There are times when a stick float must be held back – and other times when you won't catch unless it is going through your swim with the speed of the current.

A lot of people ask when to use a stick float and when to use a balsa float, and what the difference is between the two. Originally, the stick float was developed for fishing the light shotting pattern on the Trent. With a heavy bait, such as the caster, it casts well and, with the heavy cane bottom on the float, it sits well in the water, especially when you are holding it back to slow up the bait. Also, with its very buoyant tip, it was good for spotting bites, especially on the drop – that is when the fish intercepts the bait on its way down to the depth you are fishing.

It operates best in a medium flow swim which is around five to six feet deep, but imagine the same depth swim which is pulling through just that bit faster. The water is crinkled and there are small whirlpools forming – just the type of place you would

POPULAR FLOATS

expect on the River Severn. The extra power of that water would make those light shotting patterns and the work of the stick float useless.

What you need here is a balsa. The shotting pattern could be the same, but the shot would be bigger. Replace the No. 8 shot with No. 4, or even BB. The difference in the floats is that simple, all you need to do is weigh up the swims and the speed and force of the river.

Right, let's have another look at the swim to decide just how much lead your float should be carrying, once you have decided you are going to use either the balsa or the stick. This is one of the most difficult things to decide and one which you have to work out after years of experience. As a general guideline, think about using a No.6 shot every foot of depth, but always remember that a faster swim could mean a lot more shot than that, possibly even some BB bunched right down the line. As I have said, it is something you can only learn by experiment.

Remember, if you see the float lifting up a bit when it should be bullying its way through the swim, it is not big enough to do the job. It just hasn't got the right shot-carrying capacity. It is not being the master of the swim, and it is time either to go heavier or to bulk those shot down your line in the bottom third of the depth. If you bulk those shot, say two feet from your hook, then remember to have a dropper shot between them and the hook so that bites will show more positively.

Nothing is simple in fishing and, just to make things worse, there are times when fish will not stand bulk shotting. That is when you change to the bigger float, keep the same shotting pattern but use heavier shot. Now a lot of you will no doubt get the float and the shotting pattern right and then find that when you start trying to ease that float through the swim it rises in the water.

Well, to beat this, try adding an extra shot. This is a shot which is not needed to get the float to sit right in the water, in fact it will sink the float. So, to stop the float from sinking you must hold it back against the current. This not only means that you get the effect that you desire, but you also have a much more sensitive fishing rig. It takes a bit of practice, but once you have mastered it this is a great method.

As I have just said, the original stick floats we used had a cane bottom and balsa top. Nowadays, there are wire stemmed sticks

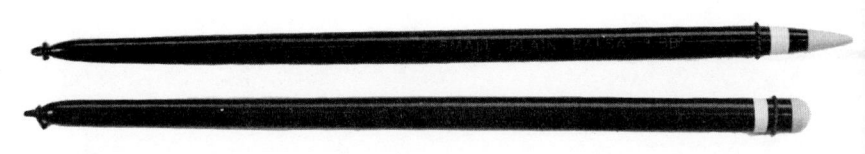

Two balsa floats, one with a normal cone top and one with a flat top

Three wire stemmed stick floats of different weights

Six stick floats of different sizes

An Avon float

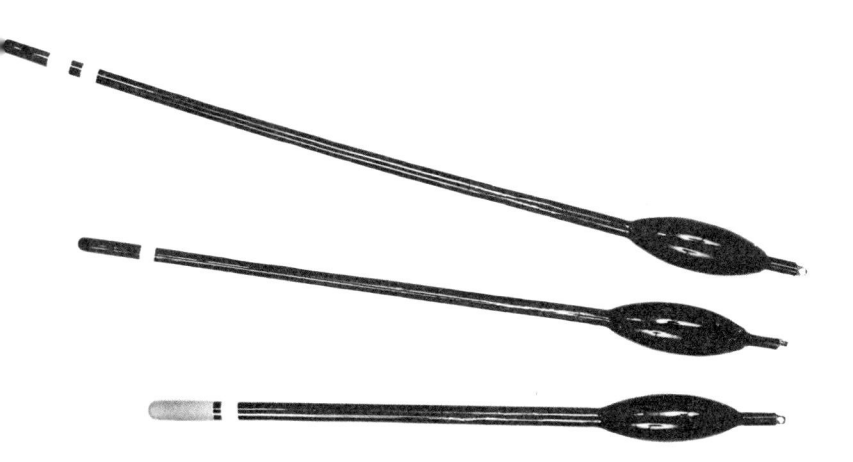

Three bodied wagglers

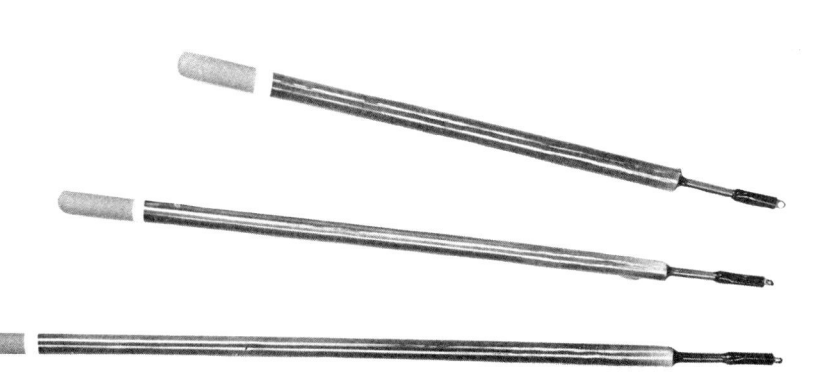

Three straight wagglers

on the market which can do just as good a job. These have a balsa body and then a long piece of rigid wire for this base. It is conventionally new compared to the others but is a very good float and can do just as good a job as the original version. These days it is becoming more common, partly because it is easier to make.

A closer look at the stick and balsa floats reveals that some of them have flat tops and others a cone type top. Personally, I don't like to use a perfect flat top; I prefer more of a broad dome because I find it easiest to get on with, particularly when using the over shotting method. With a fine conical top you have to put a slight check on it and almost let it run through with the speed of the river but, with the broader top, you can really hold the shot back which makes it an exceptionally good float for fishing over shot and overdepth. I would go for it every time.

Let's have a closer look at wagglers now. They come in two basic shapes, the bodied ones and the straight type. This type of float can be used on virtually any type of water from still to steadily-flowing venues. Basically, the bodied type are used to allow you to get more shot on the line so that you can cast greater distances. Wherever I can get away with a straight waggler that is the type I would use – and I shall tell you why.

It came after I had fished a series of matches on a lake in Staffordshire. I fished it with a straight waggler about six inches long, a foot overdepth and with just one No. 8 on the bottom, a No. 4 shot mid-water and with three BB locking the float. I was casting out around four lengths and loose feeding casters with a catapult to catch fish regularly. It was a nice day with just a ripple on the water and fishing was quite easy.

It looked as though I was on for a certain victory. But in the end I was lucky to win the match. The wind got up during the event and it made casting with this light tackle very hard work. The fish of course were still feeding in the same spot so, to make casting easier, I slipped a small cork body onto my waggler which allowed me to put even more shot on my line. This allowed me to fish a bodied waggler instead of the straight one, and I kept my shotting pattern the same by just putting all of the extra weight right under the float.

The bite came just the same when I cast in, I struck and then bounced the fish off the hook. I never gave it a second thought

POPULAR FLOATS

but after catching a couple of more fish I bounced out of a few more and I was convinced the body was responsible for this. In the end I was bouncing out of as many fish as I caught.

I went home with the idea in my head that the body on the float had been responsible. At first, I couldn't believe that it was possible, until two weeks later I fished another match on this water. Conditions were bad and I started off with a bodied float and, although I was catching, I was also losing fish – a lot of fish. I wondered straight away if the body was to blame so I took the float off and put a straight one on. It had exactly the same shotting capacity as the other one, but from then on I never lost a fish.

I have also proved this point at other times. When you are fishing in four or five feet of water and fishing with a straight waggler you will not lose as many fish as you will with a bodied float. In fact, I will not use the bodied version unless I am casting a great distance.

Staying on the subject on bodied floats let's turn to the Avon. This, to put it very simply, is like a stick float with a body. It is a very good float which is used in more turbulent water. It is designed to carry more lead than both the stick and balsa and yet it has still got the very sensitive top and is a very good float for when you are holding back. It belongs really to the balsa family.

16
Sliding floats

My float box is dominated by one particular tool which has probably won me more than any other item in my box – the loaded slider. It was this float which won me the World match and I can safely say I'm never happier than when I am using one.

I must admit that I became interested in using sliders after reading how our country's first-ever World Champion, Billy Lane of Coventry, used to fish them. But whereas Billy advocated plenty of lead on the line I prefer the loaded floats. I believe this helps people cast better and gives a better bite indication. Don't forget that with the loaded float you are in action as soon as it hits the water, unlike the usual slider which remains flat until the bulk shot comes into operation.

I used to weight my floats by wrapping and gluing lead wire to the cane base. Now, I prefer to make the base of the float from a brass rod as this makes a much cleaner finish. The weight leads to greater accuracy, less tangles and greater distance. Some of my floats are so heavy you could throw one 25 yards! As I have already said, they also allow you to fish with less lead on the line.

A lot of people, I know, are not too keen on using sliders because they fear tangles and worry whether the line will go through the bottom ring of the float. Well, my answer to this is to have a No. 12 swivel on the bottom of the float to act as an eye. The other eye of the swivel is attached to the float with a piece of 20 lb line. This allows the float to hang nice and loose when it is being cast.

Now have a look at my shotting pattern (figure 1) which shows you have only six feet of line to cast between the float and hook and also that the float will rest on the top No. 4 shot which prevents it from tangling with the bulk. When using this slider

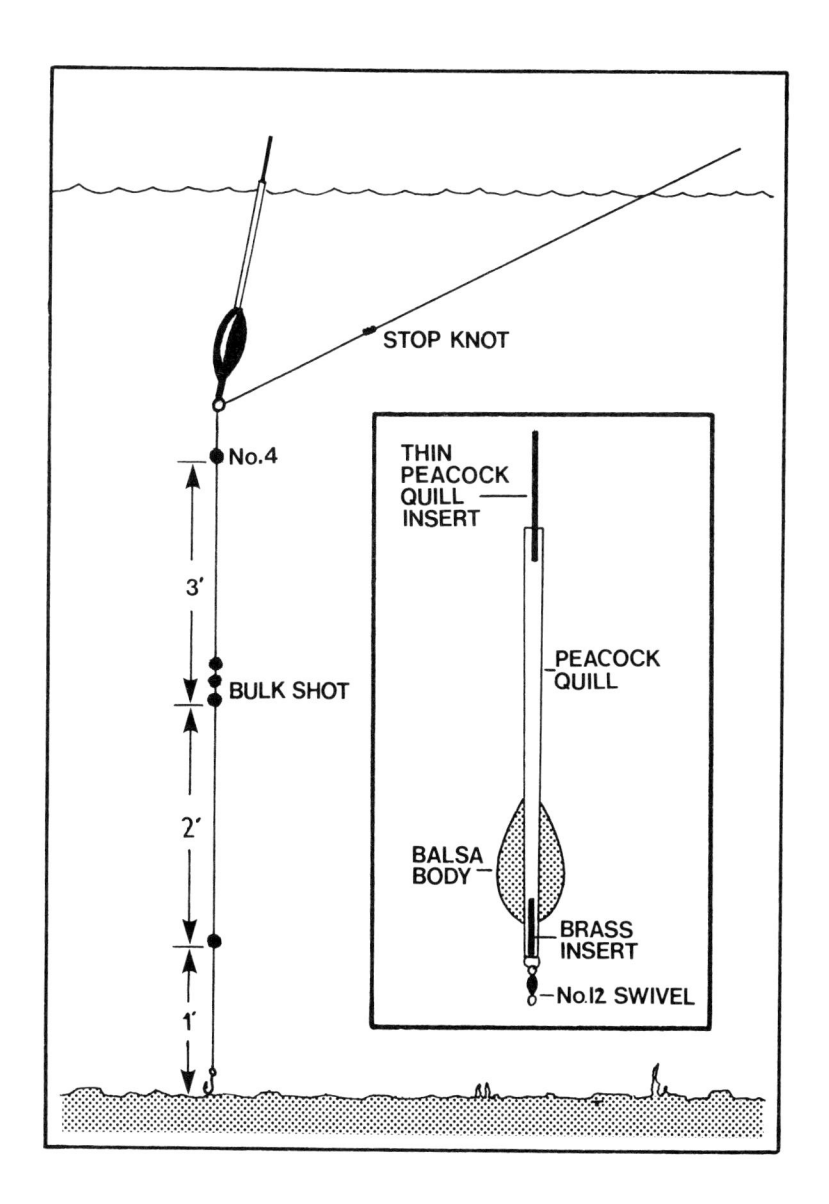

Figure 1: Ian's shotting pattern

you should put your rod top under the water and sink the line as soon as the float cocks. It will cock virtually on hitting the water because of the lead wire. This means that your line will actually be sunk whilst the rest of the shot is sinking.

Remember to count how long it takes for all of the shot to settle and cock the float down to its limit. If for some reason it does not cock in the counted time strike, as a fish has probably taken your bait on the drop. If the fish takes as soon as your float is in the water you will find that it lifts right out.

The distances I have marked between the different shots are important, but if you want your float nearer or further away from your hook then keep the shotting distances in proportion. That way you will keep tangles to a minimum.

How you cast the float has a lot to do with personal preference as overarm, sidecasting or even underarm all have their uses. I prefer to cast mine well into the air and then, just before it touches down on the surface, I will slow down the line so it hits with the minimum amount of impact and also nice and cleanly.

Don't think you have to fish these loaded floats just as sliders. You can also use them, like I did in the World match, as a waggler. Still use a stop knot at the depth you require but set it just a foot above the shot where your float will be resting when you cast. This means that when you get a bite and strike you will be striking straight into the fish and not into the float as with a normal waggler. This can make a big difference in how many bites you hit, especially at big distances.

Whilst on the subject of floats I think it is appropriate to have a few words on the topic of how much lead to use. For me, far too many people are obsessed nowadays with fishing light. All too often they do not experiment and put on enough lead. Sometimes as many as three AAA and more down the line can actually help your catch rate.

For instance, when there is an upstream wind and the water is only pushing against it slowly the key to more fish is usually a bunch of shot well down the line and just a tell-tale shot between the bulk and the hook. That bulk shot will help to hold your float in the water and will get caught in the current below the surface drift – which because of the wind is probably going in the opposite direction – and will put your float along with the current. This will mean that your bait looks more natural to the fish. After all,

It may not be the best-looking float box but Ian certainly knows how to use its contents, many of which are home-made

would you expect a fish to take a bunch of maggots which is going in a different direction to the flow?

Let's now take this step further and look at a session I once had on the Trent. It was in the days when the caster ruled supreme and delicate shotting was the order of the day. I was fishing just above Gunthorpe Bridge near Nottingham and there was a small match on the opposite bank.

That match was won with around 8 lb and dozens of anglers were moaning that their casters were coming back shelled and they hadn't spotted a bite. On this day I used a large waggler locked with two swan shot, with two AAA and a BB as a bulk shot with just a tell tale below that. The result? I had 80 lb of roach, including my best ever specimen from the river which bumped the scales to 1¾ lb. Of course there will be times when this doesn't work.

This to me is what makes the difference between a good and a bad angler. As I explain elsewhere in the book, what determines how many fish you catch depends largely on your feeding patterns, but even if you get these right you must have the shotting pattern to go with them. If you are not catching don't do the obvious and change to lighter line and smaller hooks. It could only need a change in the shotting. Moving just one shot up or down the line might make a big difference in how your bait goes along with the current and make it much more attractive to the fish.

Generally speaking, I have found that the more lead you can get on the line and still present the bait properly the more, and the bigger, fish you will catch. Obviously in summer the fish are higher in the water and more inclined to chase a bait than in winter so even for different times of the year you will have to think about changing your shotting. The only thing I can say to you so that I do not confuse you with hundreds of shotting patterns is that practice makes perfect and there is no substitute for experimenting yourself.

Ask me when the biggest turning point of my career came I have got to admit that it was after watching the match of the reels on the River Trent.

This match was between a group of anglers from Lancashire, led by Benny Ashurst, and the locals of Nottingham. Its aim was to try and show which was the best reel for the river, the centre pin

SLIDING FLOATS

or the Lancastrians fixed spools. For me it failed in that respect, but it did illustrate a point that I have never forgotten.

I knew, because at that time I was just starting to pick up regularly on the Trent, that the Lancashire lads were using the now more conventional system of stringing out small shot below their floats and fishing casters, so I decided to watch one of the Nottingham lads. But it wasn't his catch rate or his centre pin reel which interested me . . . it was the business end of his tackle.

On his line, despite the fact that he was float fishing, he had a drilled bullet and, as I noticed when he put down his rod to pick up some groundbait, his float was overshotted. This meant he was having to hold his line back hard whilst he was fishing to keep the float on the surface and in turn this meant he was slowing his bait right down.

To me the Lancashire lads were fishing too light and the Nottingham ones too heavy. The best method was obviously in between the two styles and this led to me to use a bunch of tapered shot. This bunch meant you were able to slow down the bait and, by moving it up and down the line, you could still catch the fish at different depths as they moved around the swim or came up in response to loose feed.

Shortly after this match the fish on the Trent changed the way they were feeding and my new-found method proved a winner and helped me to score regularly.

Let me give you another vital piece of information about bulk shotting. Don't think it is easier to put one big shot on the line than a few smaller shot which make up the equivalent weight. If you put on a number of smaller shot and bunch them together, you can soon space them out if the feeding pattern changes. If you have that big shot on by itself you will have to get if off the line and then find out the equivalent number of smaller shot that will suit your particular float.

17

Canals: the neglected fisheries

Ask most anglers where they would prefer to fish and they will tell you their favourite venues are on a river, or more likely a pond. But one of the most rewarding and testing venues you can ever find is likely to be a canal.

Already, I bet a lot of you are thinking that canals are only for match anglers and that they offer poor sport. I will agree with you that they are mostly used by match anglers and that in many cases they offer poor sport compared to river. But the opportunities presented by canals are far greater than you can imagine. They can test your skills to the absolute limit and make you into a much better fisherman. Being brought up on a canal myself – the Peak Forest Canal – I can vouch for that.

Obviously, it was the natural place to start for me. Like a lot of you I also got fed up with only small nets of fish from a canal and that is when I started to travel for my fishing. Now, I could fish matches on a river, get 14 lb of fish and go home happy – even if I hadn't finished anywhere.

Eventually though I realised that canals were every bit as much a part of my angling life as any other water. I admit that only in exceptional circumstances could I expect to catch as many fish from them as a river but, more important, I had to learn how to catch more fish from them than anyone else. That, as you will all agree, is what competition fishing is all about. If you are a pleasure angler only, then catching a big fish from a canal – or more than your friend – is still a challenge which I reckon is worth pursuing.

Let's now have a simplified look at what canal fishing is all about. Immediately, I bet most of you thought I was going to say you will have to fish the far side, with a float and casters as bait.

CANALS

Well, I'm sorry to disappoint you but that is just one of many ways to tackle these waters. If it is the only one you can think of then stay away – you stand no chance!

Just imagine that we are going to fish a match on a canal which is typical of many and contains mostly roach and gudgeon. The rules we apply to fishing it are just as good a guideline to you even if you are just going out for pleasure.

I think most of you will agree that at some stage during the match that shelf on the far side is going to hold fish. In fact it is probably the place where the bigger fish will be found at most venues. So, as soon as the whistle goes I would put some feed over there. Just a few casters will do, and I do mean a few, probably no more than a dozen – if that many. These have the advantage that they do not disappear into the bottom mud like maggots – but remember that when you feed again. If your first offering has not been eaten there is no point putting in some more thus leaving a big pile of food for any fish that does come along. If you put that much feed in, the chances are that the fish will eat everything and not feel like eating the bait on your hook!

Now, back to how we actually start fishing. Remember that a lot of people have walked along the bank to their pegs, but unlike a river where this will have spooked the fish and sent them off towards the middle or far bank, canal fish may well be used to this – especially if it is a busy footpath along the water – and will not necessarily be worried.

The obvious place to start fishing is at your feet. That nearside shelf is probably holding a few gudgeon or the odd bonus roach. If not, they will have dropped over the shelf and be lying hard up against it but in the deeper water.

Now, even when you have tried these places for a few fish you still have three spots left to try on the canal. You can try down the middle – (which is usually less affected by boat traffic than anywhere else if the water is deep) or at the bottom of the far bank shelf or on the far shelf itself.

When and why you should try each one of these spots is something that tends to vary from canal to canal and also in different swims. It is something that you must work out for yourself as you fish and as you learn from the venue. One thing I can tell you is that it usually pays to try a different swim – even if you are catching in one. After three or four fish in a row from one spot try casting to another, but do not stop feeding. Once a few fish have been hooked from a spot the rest of the fish more often than not get a bit wary and you can quite easily lose them unless you give them a bit of a rest. If the feed keeps going in they will eventually get all their confidence back and you can cast back to them and keep catching.

This means it is always best to keep two – or even three – spots baited up ready for the fish, just as you would on a river. Remember that important point about feeding though. There is very little, if any, flow in canals and, like stillwaters, bait is not washed away except perhaps when a big boat goes through. Try, therefore, to imagine how many fish are in your swim and how much they are eating. Too much feed will kill the spot stone dead. In fact, there will be times on canals when you will not need to feed at all to keep the fish going.

Mention the word groundbait when you talk about canals and a lot of anglers will think you are mad. Talk about using groundbait – especially when you have just told them to cut down on the feed – will make them think you are crazy. Far from it. Groundbait can be a killer, especially when those hungry little gudgeon or small roach are about.

Here again though don't forget that, just like maggots and casters, groundbait is filling to the fish, especially if wrongly mixed. Try and mix your feed so that if forms something like a milky cloud in the water. This will attract the fish and when gudgeon and skimmer bream are around it seems to inspire them into feeding. Swims that have been dead sometimes seem to spring to life with a bit of colour from the groundbait.

Cereal groundbait seems to come into its own when bread punch bait is being used on the hook. In fact, I would go so far as to say that it is a must with the punch. On a number of occasions I have seen the roach almost crawling up a pole to the bread punch – and balls of light groundbait having to be fed with every cast in to keep them interested. I saw one angler getting fish on the drop with the punch and he too was feeding the light groundbait every cast. Until he put in the groundbait he had only been getting an occasional fish.

There are times when the groundbait can also be the kiss of death on a canal, just as it can on other venues. Sometimes this has nothing to do with its feeding qualities. For example, I remember

CANALS

a friend of mine telling me a few years ago how he had ruined a good roach swim on a canal by introducing white groundbait. He had been catching a few roach on the maggot and, knowing that the cereal would probably make them come a bit faster he started feeding it.

Being a good angler he fed just the right amount – but his swim still died! What then was the reason? Believe it or not, that groundbait had attracted pike which scared everything else away. The cloud had indeed attracted the roach first but, the roach could now easily be spotted in the cloud of feed, whereas before they could not be spotted so easily in their natural background.

The pike had used the white cloud as a target area to spot the roach. In fact, there were so many pike in this canal and especially this swim, that my mate got two of them – about 5 lb each – on red maggot waggler. Before you think that was great and helped him out – I must tell you that they didn't count in this event!

Another thing about canals that I have noticed upsets a lot of anglers is the 'flow'. More often than not this flow is merely surface drift. Sometimes there is also an underflow, perhaps caused by the opening and closing of locks, and you must take all these factors into account when feeding and casting in. The feed and your tackle must all end up in the same place. On a number of occasions I have catapulted my feed out in a line immediately in front of me – and then had to cast as much as five feet to the right or left to be on top of it.

If you're not sure where your feed is landing then try casting around your swim. There are a lot of times when you will suddenly find yourself into fish after sitting there without a bite for ages. That is probably because the feed hasn't gone straight to the bottom where it hit the water.

Combating this flow – or even using it – to help you catch fish is another of the problems on these near-still waters. Most people believe that it is important to nail the bait to the bottom of the canal in order to catch a fish. That is not always the case. At times I have found that 'trotting' the drift as you would in a river also works. Obviously it is a matter of finding how the fish want the bait presenting on the day. On many occasions both methods will work during the course of a session.

The important thing to remember when you are putting the bait hard on the bottom is to keep the shotting pattern balanced to the best possible method. That is to say, make sure that the fish does not have a big weight to lift off the canal bed. Use a small amount of shot as possible. Sometimes you will find a No. 6 or No. 8 shot is quite enough.

When there is drift on the canal and you are trying to keep your bait still past the middle or over the far bank then this is where you may have problems. The 'flow' obviously pushes your float – which should be finely shotted down – under because the hook length and bottom shot are on the bed of the waterway. This is when you may have to have that little bit extra of float showing so that it does not go right under with the pull of the water – and that could mean a slightly bigger shot on the bottom so that when the fish picks up your bait the weight of the shot is used to sink the float and cannot be felt by it.

18
How to be a star

So, you want to be a top class angler? Well, unless you are prepared for a hard slog with plenty of headaches, disappointments and costly exercises you may as well stop right now.

There is no easy way to the top. Two or three good results do not make a good angler. It takes years of painstaking experience to reach any degree of consistency. There are a few 'natural' anglers around who do get there faster than others, but generally they are few and far between and they usually have the benefit of a father or other relation who is a very competent angler.

Once you have decided that match fishing is for you then you must look for the fixtures that will give you the best chance of winning. Obviously, this is going to be in the smaller club level matches, and I do mean small. Some clubs now carry a lot of talented fishermen. Even winning a 30-peg event in some of these is difficult, so choose carefully.

A few results at this level will give you the confidence and experience you need before going on to bigger matches. Consistent success at club levels will make you want to look for better competition which leads to more glory and money.

This is when you must consider carefully whether to go on to the Open circuit. In this country it is now probably harder to win on the open circuit than anywhere else in the world because of the high quality of anglers.

Six or seven years of consistency at local level does not necessarily mean instant success on the Open circuit. If you can come up with something one step ahead of other anglers – you stand the best chance.

Leeds angler Dave Thomas did just that a few years ago. Dave, who had a very good time with locally arranged matches decided to try his luck on the Trent circuit, definitely the country's hardest testing ground. He came up trumps almost immediately.

His ingredient for success? – the now famous chrysodene maggot which revolutionised fishing on the river almost overnight and left the venues top anglers having to completely re-think their outlook.

At the time Dave shot to stardom caster was king of the river. People didn't even consider maggot good enough, but Dave put all of his confidence in the bait.

Over the following five years he was never out of the limelight and his ultimate honour came in 1978 when he won the Matchman of the Year title, mostly due to the Trent and the maggot.

Dave's success can be achieved by others who can come up with something new. It might not be any method or bait new to angling; it may just be a variation on an old theme. After, all, people had used maggots for decades before Dave scored.

It is being 'one step ahead' that keeps the big-name anglers at the top. They are willing to try all new methods as they develop and, more importantly, to improve them if they are worthwhile. As I have said before, watching anglers is the best way to learn. But always try to improve on their methods rather than copy them. If you copy you can only be as good as the next man.

Experiment with anything you think might work. It doesn't have to look right or follow any of the guidelines laid down by the experts – as long as it catches fish. Some of our top anglers, Kevin Ashurst and I included, often do things that look totally wrong – until they are explained.

Remember, a lot of anglers wear blinkers when they fish the same river week in and week out. If a method has scored for long enough they will start to believe it is unbeatable. More often than not they are wrong, just like the Trent where they said maggot wouldn't beat casters.

I know another venue where the locals would only fish heavy line, big floats and big baits. Chub and bream were the quarry, and they ran big! Small hooks, light shotting patterns and loose fed maggots were useless, I was told. But once again these people were proved wrong. A friend of mine fished a match on the water, a fast flowing river, and although it was his first visit there he came second – on the 'wrong' method.

He started in the same way as the locals and soon had a bream,

Maggot ace Dave Thomas who, says Ian, changed fishing on the Trent practically overnight

but then everything went dead. Even a few casts with a swimfeeder just into the deep water about 1½ rods out failed to produce.

This was when my friend decided that due to cold water and weather the fish were probably closer in. On this line the water was that little bit slower and, because it was shallower, likely to be a bit warmer as the sun had come out. Now the locals also fished this shelf, but with the normal heavy tackle.

My friend took a gamble, which I had told him could work. He forgot about the groundbait he had been told was vital and started loose feeding maggots on the near shelf. Off came the 2½ lb line and 14 hook and heavily shotted float. On went a light stick, 1 lb line and 18 hook. The response was immediate. Bream and chub came steadily whilst the anglers around him watched amazed as they could not even manage a bite.

After the final whistle they thought he had discovered a secret bait and hurried down the bank to talk to him. When he told them the 'secret' was how he tackled the swim they wouldn't believe it – until he showed them.

It's easy to tell you what makes a good angler, in fact I can sum it up in one word, dedication. But what sickens me is when anglers keep branding others as lucky when they string together a few results. There are a few anglers around who are truly superb – yet they may not have been winning regularly for a number of years. That does not mean they have suddenly lost all their ability.

One of the biggest problems in our game is that angling is unlike any other sport. You can cast, feed and fish better than anyone in the world, but if the fish are not in your swim you cannot catch them. What you must do is fish like a world-beater all the time so that when you are not on the best pegs you still stand a chance of at least getting the prizes. I know one angler for example who just couldn't get a draw for more than two years and during that time he did not win a match. His form was incredible over that period though – he never finished less than third in his section every match, and I reckon that is consistency.

Let's look at a certain angler's case to illustrate some of these points. John Dean, from Nottingham, who in 1979–80 season won the Matchman of the Year title. During that season he had a run which was out of this world. Never a week seemed to go by without him being in the money. On the Trent circuit, where

John Dean, Matchman of the year 1979–80

John fishes, there were rumours that he had discovered a new secret or a new method. A lot of jealous anglers, whose own form left a lot to be desired, reckoned John was only drawing the best swims on the river. All of these people were wrong.

John, who has had a number of good seasons without the recognition he deserved, had just strung it all together. He had combined total dedication to the sport with a few good draws to have a dream season.

He illustrates my point perfectly, as he was winning off pegs that other people didn't rate. In fact, his form was so good that at some matches people were packing up and going home if they were pegged near him and he didn't catch straight away. They thought that if John couldn't catch what chance had they.

A few of the anglers who fish with John told me the truth though. John was just a brilliant angler. He was prepared to take the trouble to find out the winning methods for different swims. I think one summed it up perfectly when he told me that John did the same thing as everyone else – only he did everything just a little bit better.

Remember that anglers are not like footballers, cricketers or other professional sportsmen. Although we need skill we also need our fair share of luck.

19
Preparing for matches

Never go to a match stone-cold – remember that forwarned is forearmed. Once you have decided on your venue then try to discover as much about the water as you can.

Look at the results from matches there, discover which anglers finished in the frame and how they did it. Work out the tackle you need, right through the different colour floats, weights of swimfeeder and types of pole tackle. Think out all of the possible conditions, right down to the speed and direction of the wind.

Things that might seem trivial before a match and not worth bothering about could end up as the winners on the day. Little things like the thickness of your line or whether it floats or sinks.

Check your gear thoroughly for what needs to be replaced or overhauled – and don't forget that bait will eventually be the key to whether or not you catch more than the next man. Better bait catches better fish and more of them.

Order things like casters, pinkies, bloodworms in advance to make sure you get them. Make some of your own special maggots which can be killers on hard fished venues (more about that later). If you haven't the time to turn your own maggots put some shop bought ones in sugar for a few hours and this will make them a softer, cleaner hookbait.

In winter, when you use shop bought maggots, go for the long ones to put on the hook rather than the short fat ones which look better. The nicer looking ones end up going even smaller in the water and are not nearly as attractive to the fish.

Bronze maggots have been the craze over the past few years but why not try something I and a few other top anglers have. Dye your hemp. After all, if you are feeding hemp in an attempt to attract fish if it is also bronze you must stand a better chance. All that is needed is a few pinches of dye which will colour the white of the hemp after it has been cooked.

Let's have a look at that bronze maggot now. I have been told by one of my friends in the tackle business that around seven out of ten people visiting his shop now buy the chrysodene maggot.

The trend has developed so much from the match angling scene that even pleasure anglers are using the bait which seems to score on almost every venue. Obviously since the maggots are dyed they come in different shades of bronze ranging from a pale, yellowish colour (which many matchmen seem to prefer) through an orange colour to almost brown – but this darker colour doesn't seem to score so heavily.

The best way to get the colour you want is to dye the bait yourself. It's not difficult to do providing you have chosen a good maggot. Go for a soft one which is relatively fresh which allows it to hang well on the hook and wriggle about.

Riddle the maggots so they are clear of any bran or sawdust then mix the chrysodene powder – which you can buy from tackle shops – into a strong solution with water. Half a teaspoon of powder to around a pint of maggots is about right. Add more or less until you get the right shade. Add the solution to the maggots until you get the right shade and then leave for a few hours.

Then, sieve the maggots again and put them into fresh sawdust. Do this the night before a match and the maggots will look sparkling and fresh ready for use. One word of warning though. Do not wash the maggots before you dye them as this leads to them floating after being dyed.

What about breeding some of your own special maggots? Since the bait is more likely to be a bit better than the shop-bought bait it can put that few extra fish in your net when others stop catching.

It is cheap enough to get the maggots for hook bait and you can do it with very little smell. Go and buy a piece of chicken, breast will be best, and it won't cost you a small fortune. Even if you only get around a quarter of a pint of maggots you will have enough for the hook.

Buy your meat on a Friday and put it on some fresh bran in a bait box without a lid. Leave this outside to dry in the fresh air and by Saturday you should have some fly blows which are white and about the size of a small finger nail. Around two or three blows are enough.

PREPARING FOR MATCHES

When you have the blows put the lid back on the box and keep it where the temperature is not too hot or too cold. Within five days the maggots should have eaten all the meat, leaving no smell or waste. If the weather is warmer the maggots tend to come off the meat faster. When they do come off, probably around the next Friday, put them into fresh, damp bran and you are ready to go fishing.

When you use these on the hook don't forget to introduce a few into your swim with your normal maggots. Fish get a taste for them and expect more than just the one dangling on your hook to keep them interested. I have always found that this type of bait can be unbeatable when bream and roach are around.

Let's have a quick look now at tackle, just to give the beginners a bit of advice. First of all, don't buy something just because it looks good. I know a lot of youngsters and beginners buy heavy line, big hooks and lots of bait because they are under the impression they cannot catch a lot of fish, or big fish, without this gear. That is completely false.

You would be far better off buying half a pint of maggots, small hooks and light line. Provided that the float is shotted well down it

Ian's tackle box – it's a good job you don't loose points for untidiness

doesn't matter a great deal what pattern it is. The old saying about feeding small amounts of bait still applies today.

Whenever you can, knock together your own gear. Home made floats, or shop bought ones which are doctored, are often a lot better for coping with a particular job. Also if you have made your own gear you will probably feel more confident whilst using it.

Never ignore the experts. Just because they have a name behind them doesn't mean they won't talk to you. Providing you are not jumping around the bank scaring the fish most of the best anglers in this country will be only too willing to talk to you and pass on some tips.

20
Life at the top

Before I won the World Championship in 1976 I worked as a sheet metal worker at a small local firm which made superb products. There were only about 20 employees but all of the lads were first rate craftsmen and we got on really well together. When they heard I had been chosen to represent England they were almost as happy as I was.

But the management didn't seem to be too pleased by the thought that one of their employees would be representing his country in a sport. In fact, they turned their noses up a little bit when they realised I would need three or four days off work for a practice session with the rest of the team. In addition to this I would also need a few days off to take part in the match, and they seemed to take a dim view of this.

Although we were getting good money as craftsmen, the lads thought that it was wrong that I was off to represent England and yet still lose some of my wages. Unknown to me at the time, the lads got together and saw the management and said they thought that I should be compensated in some way whilst I was away, but nothing ever came of this. It was still nice to know that the lads were behind me anyway. On my way back from Poland all I could think about, believe it or not, was getting back to work to see the lads' faces now that I was the World Champion.

I treated them all to a booze-up and the champagne was flowing; they were all really happy that I had won. When I told them the win had brought me no money they seemed taken aback at first but then the champagne seemed to flow even faster. It was then that I started to get offers to open fishing tackle shops for people, for a fee, and then there were innumerable requests to attend presentation nights.

Despite the growing number of requests for teach-ins from clubs and other demands on my services, usually for a small fee, I tried not to lose any time from work but, for instance, if I was doing a forum a hundred miles from home I would try and get away just that bit earlier for the long drive. Always I took only the minimum time that I needed. This enabled me to go home and grab a quick sandwich before hurtling down the motorway to events and then getting home at ridiculous hours like two or three in the morning. Then, I would have to be up again at half past six in order to get to work on time.

The more I was in demand the greater the pressure became until at times I became too shattered to get up in the morning and was forced to have a half day off work through sheer exhaustion. Besides losing an occasional day at work I also noticed I was starting to lose my friends because they realised that I was capitalising on my win. Everything was so new to me and I made a few small mistakes. One was not keeping my mouth shut when I was offered cash to open shops and other events.

When they thought I was earning £50 for an opening, which was almost equivalent to a week's work or a good portion of it, they became rather jealous. I can't blame them really, but what they didn't think about was all the hard work that had gone in to making everything possible. I could sense I was making enemies because of my success and it wasn't very nice.

Then the management realised that the lads weren't behind me as strongly any more. By this time a year had passed and I was again selected for England – this time to fish in Bulgaria – which meant that I would again need more time off for the match and practice sessions.

During the year different fishing tackle companies had approached me to endorse their products and some of them offered really good fees. But, after weighing up the situation, I refused some large fees. I picked only the products which suited me and one of the people who I met and really got on with was Ray Field from Polynet. He had only just started his company then and although he offered me a reasonably small fee compared to some of the other companies he seemed a straightforward fellow and I liked his products.

When the management realised that I had been chosen for England again they called me in and gave me an ultimatum: I had

Ivan Marks joins Ian to show locals in Bulgaria how to catch fish, using branches as improvised rods. Other members of the team look on

to chose between being a sheet metal worker or angling. The decision was easy. There was no way I was going to let anything interfere or jeopardise my chances of representing my country and I told them that if that was the way they felt they should have my cards ready for me when I returned from the World match. When I returned they were ready.

For the first time in my life I had to sign on the dole. But, because it was classed as if I had given up my job, I was not entitled to anything for six weeks which upset me when I thought that by standing up for my country I had lost everything. When I thought of other people who were fiddling the dole it hurt just that little bit extra. Ray Field was aware of what was going on and it wasn't long before he rang me and said he wanted to see me. That phone call resulted in me being offered a directorship with the company.

Since then, I have even more demands on my time for the same

109

type of teach-ins, forums, presentation nights and other things connected with the sport and, in addition, I now look after the Northern Ireland Tourist Board's angling interests in this country. All of this has enabled me to travel the country meeting people and visiting waters I would probably never ever have seen otherwise, but my life is angling, seven days a week, 24 hours a day.

For example, let's just have a quick look in my diary. Starting on the Saturday I had a competition in Surrey which meant I had to travel there on Friday and stay overnight. I stayed in a hotel again on Saturday night so I could fish another match in the area on Sunday. On Monday I had to visit a tackle shop in the South to talk to a group of kids, then in the evening I had to present a film show for the tourist board.

Tuesday was actually a free day which meant I could go fishing, courtesy of some of the locals, but in the evening there was another forum, still in London. We left the forum late on Tuesday night and I stayed at another hotel, well outside the city, in readiness for a match on Wednesday. This was the Intrepid Sealey Masters on the River Severn at Worcester, a major spectator event. After that match I booked in to a local hotel because I had a meeting with a travel agent and the tourist board the following day.

Then it was a trip down to Hereford to meet the Welsh National team and give them a tactical talk on how to fish the River Erne where they had an international the following week. This was very rewarding as they later won the match easily. I stayed overnight in Hereford before making the journey back up country to Evesham for a practice session on Friday in readiness for the Courage invitation match on the Saturday.

After that match I travelled back to Worcester to fish another match on the Severn on Sunday and the Monday saw me back to Evesham for the Ladbroke match. Tuesday was an England practice session on a carp lake in Northamptonshire followed on Wednesday by the Southern Pole Championships on the River Lea in Hertfordshire. I finally got home on Thursday.

I am doing more fishing now than at any time in my life, but my match fishing has had to suffer a little bit. With all of my commitments, especially to teach-ins, it is impossible to compete as much as I would like. Recently, for example, I took a party of anglers over to Northern Ireland to help them improve their methods. The first day was spent showing them just where their tackle was wrong and showing them my own techniques. I probably caught about 50 lb of fish as I walked along the bank having a go with other peoples' tackle. It's surprising how much you can learn this way because you are dealing with other peoples' tackle and the shotting patterns some of them have are almost right, whilst others may have an idea you have not thought of.

On the second day of this trip the lads organised a match and invited me to take part. I won the event with 88 lb of roach and the second weight was 83 lb. That gave me a great deal of satisfaction as it proved my teaching beneficial. In fact, that night in the hotel I was asked directly if I had been trying my hardest. It was a difficult question to answer as some of the time I had been fishing as if I was taking part in the World Championships, whilst at other times I was trying out new methods.

It was then that they said that I wasn't going to win the next day and they were going all out to win. Anyway, we had a late night and didn't get to bed until after 2 a.m., which is against my normal rules for this type of match as I normally try and get eight hours sleep before an event. When I eventually got my head onto the pillow it was only for five minutes as five of them burst into the room to make sure I didn't go to sleep. This went on right through the night.

I drew a good peg the next day – and I don't know whether they had got my back up or not by keeping me up all night – but even though it was a six hour match I went on to win it with 147 lb 6 oz and the second weight was 90 lb.

A lot of World Champions – such as James Hunt – earn a fortune from their title win. It's no secret that I haven't earned huge sums of money but it hasn't made me feel bitter about the others. I love angling and never get sick of it. Of course I would have liked to have earned a lot, but I am still glad that I can say I won the title for my country and that I had the honour to represent England. I am quite happy to be in the position I am now of being able to go fishing and help organise the sport for others.

In fact, I can now organise my life around fishing, and that is good enough for me. That is worth a fortune. I am very busy, my work takes up a lot of time, but it is my sport and I am sure a lot of people must be envious that I am making a living out of something that was once a hobby. I could never go back to factory work now that I have had a taste of this.